Wreckage and Wonder

Intriguing Catastrophes and Collaborations

Michael E. Burk

Wreckage and Wonder: Intriguing Catastrophes and Collaborations
Copyright © 2025, Michael E. Burk, Annapolis, Maryland

All illustrations are original works by the author or are part of the public domain, and therefore considered free for unrestricted use.
Front cover created by the author.

Imprint: Michael E Burk Publications
Email: meburk@protonmail.com
Doc. R223 25.07.31

Disclaimer: The information in this book is accurate to the best of our knowledge at the time of publication. However, time, new discoveries, and the general chaos of history may eventually render some of it outdated or slightly inaccurate. Always consult official, reliable sources for current information. If you're considering legal action over possible errors in a historical trivia book, you might need a new hobby.

Library of Congress Cataloging-in-Publication Data
Burk, Michael
Wreckage and Wonder: Intriguing Catastrophes and Collaborations
Library of Congress Control Number: 2025910469
ISBN: 979-8-9929180-3-8 (pbk)
ISBN: 979-8-9929180-4-5 (hdbk)
1. History – Miscellanea.
2. Disasters – History.
3. Curiosities and wonders – History.
4. Technology – History.
5. Mythology – Legends.
6. Business failures – History.
7. Military history – Anecdotes.
    I. Title.
D21.W73 2025
909—dc23

Also by Michael Burk: *The Allure & The Absurd: Curious Tales from Art, Music, Film, Sports & More*

PRAISE FOR THE ALLURE & THE ABSURD:

"Michael Burk recounts bizarre, fascinating, and tragic vignettes from cultural history… with a beguiling voice that is informative, respectful when necessary, and delightfully mischievous."

– Kirkus Reviews

"A carnival where the popcorn is stale, the rides are dangerous, and yet somehow, we can't look away."

– Kirkus Reviews

"An absorbing, if often dark, compendium of stories from pop culture history."

– Kirkus Reviews

Contents

Introduction 1

Part 1 - Weirdness Abounds 4

Chapter 1 A Dancing Plague in France 6
Chapter 2 Tisquantum Piscatum 10
Chapter 3 Passenger Pigeons 13
Chapter 4 Antikythera Mechanism 15
Chapter 5 Pea-Soupers of London 17
Chapter 6 The Tunguska Event 19
Chapter 7 Who Invented Robots? 22
Chapter 8 Phineas Gage 26
Chapter 9 Nikola Tesla: Overlooked Brilliance 29
Chapter 10 Somewhere, Over in Hollywoodland 33
Chapter 11 What a Strange Trip It's Been 36
Chapter 12 The War on Sparrows 39
Chapter 13 The Tanganyika Laughter Epidemic 41
Chapter 14 The Luckiest Flight Attendant 43
Chapter 15 The Convoy Craze 46
Chapter 16 The Vampire of Sacramento 49
Chapter 17 Liquid Gold 51
Chapter 18 Mark Wahlberg and 9/11 53
Chapter 19 Daniel Tammet 54
Chapter 20 Operation Paul Bunyan 57
Chapter 21 The Würzburg Witch 59
Chapter 22 Driving While Wealthy 62
Chapter 23 Karen in the House 64
Chapter 24 The Strandbeest 67

Part 2 - Humans vs. Engineering 69

Chapter 25 The Erfurt Latrine Disaster 71
Chapter 26 The Vasa Ship Disaster 74
Chapter 27 The Tally Fire of London 76
Chapter 28 The Great Stink 79
Chapter 29 The Great Balloon Disaster 81
Chapter 30 South Fork Dam Catastrophe 83
Chapter 31 The Halifax Explosion 85
Chapter 32 The St. Francis Dam Collapse 87
Chapter 33 The Great Emu War 89
Chapter 34 USS Akron 91
Chapter 35 The New London School Explosion 93
Chapter 36 Hindenburg 95
Chapter 37 The Tacoma Narrows Bridge Collapse 97
Chapter 38 The Kyshtym Disaster 99
Chapter 39 Beach Bang Bingo: Let's Blow Up A Whale 101
Chapter 40 The Banqiao Dam Failure 103
Chapter 41 Draining Lake Peigneur 105
Chapter 42 The Gladys Positioning System 107
Chapter 43 Therac-25 109
Chapter 44 Shuttle Challenger 111
Chapter 45 The Great Balloonfest Fiasco 113
Chapter 46 The Kegworth Air Disaster 115
Chapter 47 A Chip with a Big Bug 117
Chapter 48 The Sampoong Department Store Collapse 119
Chapter 49 Columbia Disaster 121
Chapter 50 Titan Submersible 123
Chapter 51 Here Comes Another Asteroid 126

Part 3 - Collaborations and Rivals 128

Chapter 52 Murdoch & Trevithick 129
Chapter 53 Carnegie v. Rockefeller 131
Chapter 54 Charles Rolls & Henry Royce 135
Chapter 55 The Wright Brothers 137
Chapter 56 Curtiss-Wright 142
Chapter 57 Max Valier & Fritz von Opel 144
Chapter 58 Flaky Corn 146
Chapter 59 Laurel and Hardy 148
Chapter 60 Vidal v. Buckley 152
Chapter 61 Bill Murray and Chevy Chase 154

Part 4—Myth and Mystery 156

Chapter 62 The Tale of Medusa and the Gorgons 157
Chapter 63 St Patrick 159
Chapter 64 The Pied Piper of Hamelin 161
Chapter 65 The Most Mysterious Manuscript 163
Chapter 66 The Fountain of Youth 165
Chapter 67 King Arthur and the Sword in the Stone 167
Chapter 68 Bigfoot/Sasquatch 169
Chapter 69 The Mysterious Bermuda Triangle 172
Chapter 70 The Wendigo 174
Chapter 71 The Loch Ness Monster 176
Chapter 72 Mothman vs. Goatman 179

Part 5—Business Blunders 182

Chapter 73 Edsel 183
Chapter 74 Corvair 186
Chapter 75 Preston Tucker 188

- Chapter 76 Sony Betamax 190
- Chapter 77 Not MS-DOS 192
- Chapter 78 Ford Pinto 194
- Chapter 79 New Coke 196
- Chapter 80 Apple's Newton 198
- Chapter 81 Kodak's Digital Camera Hesitation 200
- Chapter 82 Blockbuster vs. Netflix 202
- Chapter 83 Yahoo Missed Google 204
- Chapter 84 The Peugeot 1007 205
- Chapter 85 Toyota Gas Pedal Recall 207
- Chapter 86 The Nokia Smartphone Decline 209
- Chapter 87 Samsung Galaxy Note 211
- Chapter 88 Theranos 213
- Chapter 89 The Volkswagen Emissions Scandal 215

Part 6 – War and/or Peace 217

- Chapter 90 Andersonville 219
- Chapter 91 Blue Hawaii 221
- Chapter 92 Play Football, Not War 223
- Chapter 93 Sniper vs. The Red Baron 226
- Chapter 94 The Giant Panjandrum 229
- Chapter 95 Bat Bombs 231
- Chapter 96 Pigeon-Guided Missiles 233
- Chapter 97 Surviving Atomic Explosions 235
- Chapter 98 A Monopoly Game Of Mass Escape 237
- Chapter 99 Maginot Line 239

Bibliography 241

END NOTES 248

Introduction

This is my second trivia book, if that's what we can call it. My first was *The Allure & The Absurd: Fascinating Tales from Art, Music, Film, Sports & More*, specifically addressing various aspects of entertainment.

Or maybe these are history books; though it's a sort of history that doesn't care too much about neat categories or rigid chronology. Some might call it a hybrid: part history, part trivia, but unafraid to venture into realms of science, engineering, and the occasional eccentric figure or two. So, let's not get bogged down in labels. It's whatever you need it to be.

As for the content, brace yourself for a veritable smorgasbord. There's absurdity galore, of course; those moments when history just refuses to behave. But it's not all lighthearted and goofy. Between the delightful oddities, you'll find tales that run the full spectrum of human experience: fascination, wonder, and, yes, more than a few heavy doses of sadness. Some stories wade into that melancholy territory, and while they might leave a lump in your throat, they don't linger in misery. The twist? They often leave behind a strange, bittersweet joy, the kind that stirs your soul enough to remind you how odd it is that tragedy and triumph are sometimes just two sides of the same coin. You might even find, as I did during my research and writing, that some of these real-life tales made me laugh—and cry—without really knowing where the tears came from.

But that's the beauty of these stories: they're unpredictable. It's the *weirdness* of life that gives them their power. The unanticipated "A-ha!" moments that turn simple anecdotes into something more, something raw and real. And, yes, you'll certainly find moments of levity. When absurdity strikes, I'll be less than serious, always looking for a laugh, even if that laugh comes at our own expense. Perhaps a dash of Groucho Marx, or the sharp, often scornful wit of

Jon Stewart. Yet, for the moments of grief and loss, I've tried to offer more than a modicum of respect. The world isn't always a place for jokes, and sometimes, just sometimes, the right tone demands a little solemnity. There are no easy answers in tragedy, no tidy little morals to be taken home, but we try to be human about it.

So, as you dive into these pages, I hope you'll find yourself occasionally laughing out loud or shaking your head in disbelief, muttering, "I didn't know that!" or, better yet, exclaiming, "That's so *wild!*" Life isn't always about the happy ending; sometimes it's just about the strangeness of it all. And whatever the emotional toll these stories take on you, whether it's tears of joy, or tears of sorrow, don't worry. You're in good company. Just make sure to laugh at the bizarre. We could all use a little more of that.

About the author

Michael E. Burk is a retired NASA Systems Engineer. He assisted with the initial design for the guidance, attitude, and navigation control systems for the James Webb Space Telescope, and worked on many deep-space projects such as the Cassini mission to Saturn, and missions to comets and asteroids. He is a contributor to the journal *Free Inquiry, French Entrée* magazine and others. He is an inventor, editor and author of over 60 articles and a dozen books. Mr. Burk spent most of his life in the United States, and now lives in the south of France.

Sources

We've included footnotes and endnotes to topics that one might find dubious, as in "I'm not sure I believe this zany tale," and especially to the chapters involving religion, because people can sometimes allow their feelings and childhood indoctrination to cloud their judgment. We have researched these topics thoroughly, and to the best of our knowledge, it's all accurate, our editorial and sarcastic comments notwithstanding. And for most chapters, we've suggested some *"Further Reading"* and *"Easy Viewing."*

Also by Michael E. Burk:

The Allure and The Absurd: Fascinating Tales from Art, Music, Film, Sports and More.

Eat, Drink, Panic: A Journey Through the Bizarre, Delicious, and Disastrous.

Retire in France by the Numbers: A Detailed Guide and Checklist.

Complete Handbook for Driving In Europe: Guidelines for all 51 Countries.

A Glimpse Beyond: The Future of Science and Technology.

Part 1 - Weirdness Abounds

In its more dignified moments, history would like you to believe it's a serious, orderly account of humanity's progress: wars fought, nations built, geniuses celebrated, treaties signed with elegant quill pens. But if you spend enough time with it, you realize it's less of a grand epic and more of an unedited blooper reel, full of strange detours, regrettable decisions, and baffling occurrences that no one ever quite managed to explain.

For instance, there have been occasions when entire groups of people lost their collective grip on reality, sometimes by laughing uncontrollably, sometimes by dancing until they dropped, and occasionally by electing deeply unqualified individuals to positions of immense power (though that last one is less of an anomaly and more of a tradition). Elsewhere, history is littered with ambitious ideas that should never have made it past the cocktail-napkin phase: proposals so spectacularly misguided that one suspects they were the result of an intellectual experiment gone horribly wrong, or at the very least, a bad case of lead poisoning.

Then there are the accidental heroes, those individuals whose claim to fame involved the sort of improbable circumstances that make you question whether the universe occasionally gets drunk and starts improvising. Some dodged death with such absurd frequency that even bad luck seemed to take it personally. Others managed to stumble into history simply by being in the worst possible place at the most inconvenient time. And, of course, we must pay tribute to the more institutional absurdities: the laws, policies, and general bureaucratic misadventures that suggest human civilization has been operating on a dare for quite some time.

Part 1 of this book is devoted to those moments when reality, seemingly unsatisfied with predictability, takes a sharp left turn into the bizarre. These are the stories that make you shake your head, squint at the page, and mutter, "Well, that can't possibly be true." And yet, here they are, standing as proof that history is not merely written by the victors, but occasionally by whoever happened to be holding the pen when something ridiculous happened.

Chapter 1 A Dancing Plague in France

Summer's Here and the Time is Right for Dancing...

How would you describe Strasbourg in the sweltering summer of 1518, entangled in the web of early Renaissance Europe? I've been there several times, it's a lovely city, peaceful, safe, even quixotic. But I don't have a DeLorean, nor a flux capacitor, so this was recently for me, not sixteenth century. And I didn't do any dancing a far as I recall.

That year, over five centuries ago, amidst such sweltering heat in Strasbourg's summer, was born something odd and profoundly disturbing: the beginning of what was to be a general breakdown that belied all rational explanation of the time. A woman was the first to dance down the streets, one whose name is lost in history (if I had to guess, Gretchen and Geneviève come to mind), though the pattern that commenced by her dancing has remained a maddening puzzle over which one could easily lose his or her reason. That first woman (let's go with "Geneviève") stepped into the streets, dancing without music, celebration, or a flicker of joy, pouring sweat from every pore and moving beyond the bounds of rhythm into an uncontrolled frenzy; the movements unrelenting, mechanical, with a soul trapped somehow in what could only be perceived as an external force. She danced under a tormenting compulsion. Picture Prince or Mick Jagger on acid. Or more appropriately (since "Geneviève" was a woman), Nina Hagen or Lady Gaga.

And this, one suspects, must have been only the beginning. It is tempting to consider it an isolated case of insanity, a momentary aberration. But it went on to engulf the city in an epidemic of motion that, from all evidence, erupted spontaneously. Others, at first unwillingly, then with full abandon, joined Geneviève Gaga. The streets became filled with an orchestra of limbs writhing in totally involuntary synchrony, some seemingly in desperation, some simply lost in the rhythm. It was not a celebration but rather a compulsion—

some sort of mass charming virus enacted upon the community—a quiet infection far subtler than physical contagion.

At first, the authorities dismissed the spectacle as mere madness, a fleeting, temporary breakdown of social norms. *Damsels Gone Wild* one might say, although the event was apparently co-ed. But soon, it became evident that this was no trivial display, no outburst born of personal hysteria. Physicians and religious figures, clutching their superstition like a talisman against the unknown, proposed diagnoses ranging from the psychoanalytic to the supernatural. "Hot blood," they declared, a theory so quaint and utterly divorced from the reality of physiological function, it might have been conjured from the fevered imagination of a medieval healer attempting to make sense of an ungovernable reality. Yet in their desperation, they built stages and hired musicians, absurdly hoping that control over the music—this most primal of human expressions—might somehow exorcise the madness. What transpired, however, was only an amplification of the original affliction. The dancing throng, maddened and exhausted, kept moving, their feet literally bleeding, their bodies crushed by the unrelenting burden of motion, until many collapsed from exhaustion, or some even worse fate.

We are left, then, with an event that pushes at the boundaries of our understanding.

Theories abound, but none of them are fully satisfying. Was it, as some suggest, a case of mass hysteria, an uncontainable psychological contagion sparked by the crippling anxieties of famine, plague, and religious fervor? Was this a collective, unconscious cry for relief amidst the suffocating pressures of the age? Or, as others postulate, did something more material, something deeply chemical, poison the people of Strasbourg: ergot, the hallucinogenic fungus that flourishes on rye, capable of inducing a delirium akin to a bad acid trip, sending them into a kind of collective fugue state, their minds and bodies overwhelmed?

No answer is definitive. Each theory, while compelling in its own way, ultimately falls short of explaining the full scope of the phenomenon. And yet, the event carries profound lessons about human psychology and physiology, about the vulnerability of the mind when subjected to extreme stress. We may marvel at the complexity of the human brain in response to such environmental pressures; neuroscientists remind us that our minds are not immune to the external forces of circumstance, or even to the very substances we consume without understanding their full impact.

But what is undeniable is that the Dancing Plague of 1518 is a ghastly reminder that, however wise and developed humanity prides itself to be, it is still exposed to unseen forces: nature's, and forces of the mind. What starts as singular anomaly becomes later something admittedly more disturbing: a social contagion that cannot be stopped, an event whose ripples still reverberate through the centuries, testimony, bizarre, to the lability of the body and manipulativeness of the mind. Simple "mob mentality"? Who knows.

In the end, the dancers collapsed or disappeared only leaving bits of their story, those bits disconnected and incomplete, a whisper of a mystery that will perhaps never be fully solved. A story that confronts the limits of human understanding, revealing how the mind and body can turn on each other under pressure, and the chilling perhaps that under such conditions, the mind itself is for us the most terrifying force we have yet to learn to reckon with.[1]

And all this happened because of one woman: Lady Geneviève! That demonic, dizzy, dancing damsel. Or Gretchen. Whatever.

Or, perhaps, some hallucinatory fungus in their food? (See the similarly zany tale on page 36.)

(Artist's conception)

Chapter 2 Tisquantum Piscatum

The Man, the Myth, the Extremely Confused Pilgrims

Tisquantum, better known to history as Squanto, was not your average 17th-century New Englander. For one thing, he actually knew what he was doing. This alone made him an outlier among the bewildered and scurvy-ridden Europeans washing up on America's shores, convinced that buckle hats and religious fervor (or escape therefrom) were adequate substitutes for survival skills. That Squanto managed to be both a victim of European expansionism and its most improbable savior is a plot twist that history, in its perpetual absurdity, delights in serving up.

If you've seen the film *Squanto: A Warrior's Tale*, prepare to learn what *actually* happened.

Some sources suggest Squanto was first taken to England around 1605, kidnapped and taken to England, where he lived for several years and learned English. The film left out his various trips through Europe, including a second kidnapping in 1614. An English trader named Thomas Hunt, whose name belongs in the great pantheon of historical villains who saw kidnapping and human trafficking as a viable business model, decided Squanto would make a fine addition to the thriving Atlantic slave trade. Off he went to Spain (along with about 20 other Native Americans whom Hunt had discovered), where he was promptly sold into bondage, because European explorers at the time had a peculiar habit of "discovering" things that already existed and then putting a price tag on them.[2]

Unlike the film portrayal, there's no evidence that Squanto was forced into gladiator-style fights or made a dramatic escape. In what can only be described as an early instance of divine irony, it was a group of Catholic friars—representing the very religion often complicit in conquest—who decided that perhaps, just this once, forcibly relocating people across the ocean to be sold wasn't a great look. They secured his freedom, at which point Squanto embarked on a wildly improbable tour of Europe, ending up in back in England. There, he improved his English language skills, which turned out to be remarkably useful later when he needed to inform the Pilgrims that, no, praying over a frozen dirt patch would not, in fact, make food grow.

By 1619, he had finally arranged passage back to America, only to discover that, in the grand tradition of history being a never-ending series of gut punches, his entire tribe had been wiped out by a European disease they never saw coming. He was now a man with no people, a Native American fluent in the language of his oppressors, caught between worlds in a way that was both uniquely tragic and darkly comedic, if one has the sort of sense of humor required to stomach early colonial history.

Enter the Pilgrims. These were not the hardy, self-reliant pioneers of mythic imagination. No, these were people who had managed to cross an entire ocean only to find themselves wholly unprepared for the most basic elements of staying alive. Squanto, ever the pragmatist, assessed their situation and likely concluded that watching them starve to death would be both morally dubious and, more importantly, tedious. So he did what any reasonable person would do: he taught them how to plant corn, how to fish, and generally not die; a set of skills that one would assume they might have considered learning before embarking on this grand escapade.

Beyond serving as a survival consultant, Squanto also became the Pilgrims' de facto ambassador to the Wampanoag Confederacy, particularly to their leader, Massasoit. This role required a degree of diplomacy that can only be described as superhuman, as Squanto had to convince the Wampanoag that these bumbling newcomers were worth keeping alive while simultaneously ensuring that the Pilgrims didn't misinterpret routine tribal customs as cause for immediate panic and musket-waving.

It was not all simple benevolence. Squanto was a smart man dealing in a complex, high-stakes game of survival, influence, and opportunism, and he operated like a bookie or hedge fund manager in buckskin. He benefited from being the intermediary between the two factions, regardless of the transactions or agreements.

And thus, through his improbable journey across continents, through slavery, survival, and a return to a homeland that no longer existed, Squanto became one of history's most reluctantly important figures. He was neither saint nor traitor, neither wholly indigenous nor remotely European: an in-between figure in an era that had little room for ambiguity. His life was proof that history, much like nature, does not conform to simple narratives. It is messy, unpredictable, and often darkly comedic in ways that would be hilarious if they weren't so horrifying.

In the vast, indifferent sweep of history, we are left with one enduring image: a lone Patuxet man standing among a group of bewildered English settlers, explaining, probably with some measure of exasperation, that if they didn't figure out how to grow corn, they were all going to die.

Squanto passed away in 1622, just a year after the famous first Thanksgiving.

— Further Reading —

Philbrick, Nathaniel, *Mayflower: A Story of Courage, Community, and War.* Viking, 2006.

Baker, William Avery, *The Pilgrim Colony: A History of New Plymouth, 1620–1691.* Yale University Press, 1961.

Chapter 3 Passenger Pigeons

This Bird Has Flown

Passenger pigeons were, once upon a time, the ornithological equivalent of an all-you-can-eat buffet that had somehow grown wings. These were not rare, delicate birds that required careful conservation; they were airborne mobs. They flapped through North America in such absurdly large numbers that people swore the sun would vanish when they passed overhead. It's possible they were exaggerating, but then again, with estimates of 3 to 5 billion birds in circulation, they may well have been understating the situation.

And yet, because humans have an uncanny ability to look at "too much of a good thing" and decide to fix it with wholesale destruction, we managed to exterminate the entire species in less time than it takes a reality TV star to wear out their welcome.

How to Ruin a Billion-Pigeon Empire

Passenger pigeons were easy to hunt, mostly because they had no natural inclination to get out of the way. They traveled in massive, feathery hordes, which meant if you fired your state-of-the-art 17th century blunderbuss in any random direction, you were bound to hit a bunch of them. Entire industries sprang up around this limitless feathered resource, because why not turn them into cheap meat, sell them for sport shooting, and maybe even grind a few up for fertilizer while we're at it? And since conservation was not a widely embraced concept at the time—this being the same era when people thought arsenic made for a fun face cream—nobody worried much about whether passenger pigeons could run out.

Adding insult to extinction, their nesting grounds were systematically destroyed to make room for farms, cities, and presumably a great many places selling pigeon meat. Worse still, these birds had a curious survival strategy: they thrived in massive numbers. If you reduced their population to smaller, more "manageable" sizes, they stopped breeding effectively. Which is a bit like saying a city can't function unless every single citizen is out on the streets at the same time. As a survival strategy, it left something to be desired.

Exit, Stage Left

By the time someone finally raised a concerned eyebrow and muttered, "Hey, should we maybe not shoot all of them?" It was far too late. The last confirmed wild passenger pigeon was unceremoniously gunned down in 1901, in a moment that was almost certainly not met with the reflective sadness it deserved. The final, solitary representative of the species, a captive pigeon named Martha, expired in the Cincinnati Zoo in 1914, marking the official moment when one of nature's most successful birds turned into history's favorite ecological cautionary tale.

What We (Hopefully) Learned

The extinction of the passenger pigeon stands as one of those moments where future generations look back and say, "You did WHAT?" It's right up there with leaded gasoline and radioactive toothpaste in the annals of staggeringly bad ideas. These birds weren't wiped out by natural disaster or some complex environmental shift; they were obliterated because humans did what humans do best: assumed that if something is plentiful today, it will be plentiful forever.

Today, the passenger pigeon exists only in textbooks, museums, and the occasional expensive genetic resurrection project, as scientists try to undo the blindingly obvious mistake of our ancestors. Meanwhile, other species teeter on the edge of a similar fate, leaving us with an important question: Will we actually learn from this? Or will we just find something new to shoot into oblivion?

— Further Reading —

Schorger, A. W., *The Passenger Pigeon: Its Natural History and Extinction*. University of Wisconsin Press, 1955.

Chapter 4 Antikythera Mechanism

A Clockwork Solar System

Picture this: it's 1901, and a bunch of Greek sponge divers—whose job, by the way, involves holding their breath for terrifyingly long stretches while prying stubborn sea creatures off of rocks—come across something even more surprising than a disgruntled squid. They find a shipwreck. Not just any shipwreck, but one that has been quietly decomposing on the seafloor for over 2,000 years. And inside it, amid the usual assortment of antiquated bric-a-brac, they pull out a corroded hunk of metal that, upon first glance, appears to be the world's most aggressively neglected pocket watch.

Fast-forward a bit, and scientists start scraping away the centuries of rust and gunk, only to discover something completely nuts. This wasn't just another rusty artifact. This was a precision-engineered, gear-driven analog computer built by people who, if we're being honest, we thought were too busy sculpting marble gods and arguing about stoicism to invent mechanical astronomy.

The Antikythera Mechanism, as it was later dubbed, turned out to be an intricate system of interlocking gears, precisely cut to track celestial motions. It predicted the positions of the sun and moon, modeled the uneven motion of the lunar orbit, and could even forecast eclipses. Which, in ancient Greece, was about as close as you could get to divine omniscience without actually declaring yourself a god and hoping Zeus didn't take offense.

Here's where it gets weirder: this level of mechanical sophistication wouldn't be seen again until at least the 14th century. So either the ancient Greeks had an undiscovered fraternity of mad genius watchmakers, or we've been drastically underestimating their ability to tinker with bronze and make the universe behave in ways that seem suspiciously Newtonian, even if it was built to model a universe with Earth stuck at the center.

And just to twist the knife a little, nobody knows who built it, how many there were, or why nothing else like it survived. Was it an isolated act of brilliance? The remnant of some lost tradition of advanced engineering? A one-off project built by an eccentric Greek who thought predicting planetary motion would be a good way to impress people at dinner parties? We don't know. What we do know is that 2,000 years ago, somebody figured out how to build a machine that, in a just world, should have gotten them the kind of historical recognition usually reserved for emperors and inventors of indoor plumbing.

Instead, it sat on the ocean floor for two millennia, waiting for some sponge divers to find it. Which, frankly, feels like a bit of an oversight on history's part.

— Further Reading—
Marchant, Jo. *Decoding the Heavens: A 2000-Year-Old Computer—and the Century-Long Search to Discover Its Secrets.* Da Capo Press, 2009.

— Easy Viewing —
BBC, "Antikythera Mechanism: The ancient 'computer' that simply shouldn't exist." (duration: 6:53) www.youtube.com/watch?v=qqlJ50zDgeA

Chapter 5 Pea-Soupers of London

Send Lawyers, Guns, and Gas Masks

No, it's not a Weird Al Yankovic parody of a Warren Zevon song. London, 19th century, was a city powered by coal. Homes, factories, and the increasingly popular railways all relied on the black nuggets for heat and energy. Coal was how the Industrial Revolution realized its dream, and its smoke perpetually permeates every nook and cranny in the city. From this inconsolable burning, the "pea-soupers" came: opaque, suffocating fogs that draped London, especially in the cooler months of the late 1800s. Not weather events but rather death smog: storms that have a foregone history of toxic alchemy between industrial activity and coal combustion with stagnant cold air. Their presence is inescapable, a dark reminder of a city powered by fuel at any cost, including human lives.

Stink.
The real horror was not just the oppressive suffocation of the fog, but what it hid; it reeked of poison. Factories, homes, and railways in the city poured out an invisible concoction of sulfate, carbon monoxide, and nitrogen oxides: chemical apparitions of the industrial age. So when a fog came over, it became very easily added to the moisture there, and its very poisonous soup: the boundaries between air and poison became rather blurred. Oh, the humidity! Thus, a noxious yellow-green vapor covered the city, almost to cast a dark shroud of condemnation over the city as though it was nearer to crumbling than flourishing.

Even the strongest men can lose their balances by smelt: the air reeked of burning sulfur, rotting organic waste, and sickly chemical fumes—a miasma that didn't just irritate the lungs but aged them prematurely. Stepping within this air is indeed an attack, not mere nuisance, on the unfortunate one's life. The fog didn't merely cloud the vision; it seeped into the skin, settling in the hair, clothing, and lungs like a persistent, toxic shadow. But worse still was the insidious nature of the smog. The consequences of inhaling this foul air were not immediately clear, but over time, respiratory issues, chronic coughing, and long-term lung damage became the silent killers. It was a slow, invisible death, a creeping tragedy waiting to unfold in full view, though many would not live to see its horrors fully revealed.

Stank.

But, in fine suffocating air, it interwove with the identity of London. It would seem that the people of the place had groaned under a burden to carry this, making it part of the world in which they played their lives. It was not merely poisonous; it was one of the hallmarks of Victorian living. Authors such as Charles Dickens used this fog to symbolize the murkiness of the time. In his novel *Bleak House*, fog was not just physical, but metaphorical: it entered the mind with senses of societal malaise, mirroring the dehumanizing forces of industrialization.

Stunk.

By the end of the century, the full scale of the danger was becoming apparent, but the seeds of this environmental catastrophe had already been sown. Though the worst of the smog would emerge later in the 20th century, the grim roots of that disaster lay in the 19th-century fogs, thick with smoke and sulfur. The pea-soupers were more than a mere nuisance; they were the heavy, oppressive mark of a world striving for progress at any cost—an industrial nightmare that would take generations to untangle, and still others to truly understand.

The Clean Air Act of 1956 was passed by Parliament in response to these pea-soupers and a later event, the Great Smog of 1952.

— Further Reading —

Brimblecombe, Peter, *The Big Smoke: A History of Air Pollution in London since Medieval Times*. Routledge, 1987.

Jackson, Lee, *Dirty Old London: The Victorian Fight Against Filth*. Yale University Press, 2014.

Chapter 6 The Tunguska Event

And It Burns, Burns, Burns

Just like any other day in the rather remote wilderness of Siberia, the morning of June 30, 1908, came with one glaring difference: it was the moment the universe unleashed a force that would echo through history. In an instant, an incomprehensibly tremendous explosion completely obliterated Tunguska's dense forest, flattening a sizeable zone of trees extending for almost 2,000 square kilometers: an area so vast that whole countries could be swallowed in it. It left 80 million trees uprooted as if swept away by a hand that cannot be seen. The very air was trembling, reverberating under the spell of an invisible force, which reached far beyond the center of the explosion, blasting shockwaves that shattered windows over 600 kilometers away.

Without warning, a column of light flared across the heavens, followed moments later by a violent concussion that flattened trees across more than two thousand square kilometers. There was no crater. No shattered rock face. Just a strangely vacant epicenter, as if the Earth had recoiled from whatever visited it.

By most contemporary records, no one perished. Some later accounts suggest a handful of casualties, but nothing definitive has surfaced, as the region was sparsely populated. In human terms, it was a near miss. In scientific terms, a turning point. The explosion, though terrestrial in location, felt extraterrestrial in nature. It arrived unbidden, left no clear evidence of its origin, and compelled a century of speculation.

For years, the origins of the explosion shrouded themselves in an obscurity as thick as the forests it destroyed. At first, it was believed that the explosion originated from volcanic activity; perhaps, one such long-forgotten caldera erupted. Yet, no volcanic signatures were found. Also dismissed was the notion of an atmospheric anomaly or unexplained natural phenomenon. But as the scientific community gazed up, the idea continued to gain traction that it was a celestial visitor. A comet or asteroid may have been the true culprit; its exact identity and composition shrouded within uncertainty. But, they reasoned, where was the impact? Where was the crater? The absence of such a decisive marker only deepened the mystery.

Finally, in 1927, a team of Soviet scientists led by L.K. Kulik ventured inside the very center of the destruction. The desolation of the scene that met them was so otherworldly: trees uprooted and blackened; the forest reduced to an empty wasteland, yet no crater, no trace of an impact. Through extensive investigation, however, the team came to a rather disconcerting conclusion: the blast's cause was a massive, aerial detonation of an asteroid or comet 50 to 60 m in diameter. The energy released was estimated in the staggering range of 10 to 15 megatons of TNT; far, far more powerful than the atomic bombs that decimated Japan, just a few decades later. From what was once supposed to be a scientific curiosity, all now appears to have revealed itself as a cosmic near miss.

Nor did the true impact of the event stop there. The force of the explosion caused the terrestrial lower atmosphere to oscillate for a while, while it experienced a momentary but unmistakable reduced temperature. This was an indication of the vulnerability of life on Earth and of how much exposed to the forces we quite can't comprehend.

The Tunguska Event, with hindsight, stands quite stark as a reminder of the cosmic forces that silently hang in the dark darkness of space to threaten us year in year out. It makes us face the vulnerability of our planet, of the thin veil of atmosphere that protects us, and above all, the unpredictable face of the universe itself. One hundred years after that explosive morning, the Tunguska Event is more than a mere curiosity and is, instead, an ongoing symbol of the unknown hazards circling just out of our grasp and constantly reminds us that, in this fragile dance through the cosmos, danger often comes unannounced.

— Further Reading —

Baxter, Stephen, and David Atkinson, *Tunguska: The Final Answer*. Faber & Faber, 2013.

Kride, E. L., *The Tunguska Meteorite: An Eye-Witness Account*. Progress Publishers, 1967.

Chapter 7 Who Invented Robots?

I, for One, Welcome Our New Cybernetic Overlords

One of history's most delicious ironies is that the term robot—now so aptly synonymous with tireless efficiency—was invented by a chain-smoking Czech playwright with bad lungs and worse luck. Karel Čapek, a Czech intellectual who was not enamored with totalitarianism and was unfortunately prone to bouts of pneumonia, coined the word in his 1920 play *R.U.R.* (*Rossumovi Univerzální Roboti*, or *"Rossum's Universal Robots"*). The word itself was suggested by his brother Josef (because what are siblings for, if not stealing your linguistic thunder?), derived from the Czech *robota*, meaning forced labor. And yet, in the grand tradition of science fiction being a little too on the nose, humanity has spent the last century turning Čapek's grim speculation into a corporate business model.

(Remember, if you discuss him with anyone, pronounce it right. The caret over the *Č* results in a "ch" sound. So his name is pronounced KAH-rell CHAH-pek.)

The robots of R.U.R. were no clinking, clanking, caliginous contraptions; they were bioengineered laborers, grown from synthetic protoplasm and stamped with a humanlike face that seemed frozen in perpetual neutrality, like an expressionless cyborg zipped into a snug Eggar suit,[a] designed to shoulder the drudgery of human civilization without a flicker of doubt or desire. This, in itself, was an act of remarkable foresight. Čapek essentially anticipated not only artificial intelligence and genetic engineering but also the entire tech industry's business plan: "Hey, let's build something smarter

---

[a] ...but without the overalls.

than us and then be surprised when it doesn't want to take our nonsense anymore." Predictably, in the play, the robots eventually realize that serving humans is about as fulfilling as being a middle manager in a company that holds trust falls instead of giving raises. They rise up, overthrow their overlords, and (spoiler alert) eradicate humanity. Like the Kaylon tried to do in *The Orville.*

A Man at Odds with His Own Lungs

Čapek was more than just an early prophet of technological revolt; he was also a first-rate thorn in the side of authoritarian regimes. He loathed both fascism and communism with equal enthusiasm, a position that earned him a spot on Nazi blacklists and guaranteed that both extremes of the political spectrum found him deeply, let's say, "inconvenient." He was a man who believed that grand ideas mattered, that words could shape history; and, judging by the fact that the Nazis banned his books, they apparently agreed.

By the late 1930s, as Europe careened toward the bloodbath he had so clearly foreseen, Čapek was a leading voice in Czechoslovakia's cultural life: so respected that some even imagined him as presidential material. He declined formal political roles, presumably because he was well aware that leading a nation at the doorstep of Hitler's Germany was about as appealing as being the designated driver at a demolition derby sponsored by Stolichnaya. His health was already deteriorating—likely from the exhausting work of yelling at people to take the rise of fascism seriously—and in December 1938, pneumonia took him before the Nazis could. Which was, if nothing else, efficient timing on his part.

Remaining Relevant

Čapek, like all good satirists, had the misfortune of being absolutely right. His robots, designed for menial labor, treated as disposable, and ultimately fed up with humanity's nonsense, now exist in the form of factory machines, experimental humanoid robots and mechanical dogs,[b] and customer service chatbots that make us yearn for the sweet release of extinction. His warning about the dehumanizing force of unchecked technological progress remains as pertinent now as it was a century ago, which is unfortunate because, as a species, we are nothing if not committed to ignoring good advice.

Even beyond robotics, Čapek's broader fears—of authoritarianism, of political apathy, of human beings blithely marching toward their own undoing—continue to haunt the present. He saw a world where technology outpaced ethics, where power corrupted absolutely, and where people, given the choice between preserving democracy and binge-watching *The Bachelor*, would inevitably reach for the remote. And yet, his works endure. *R.U.R.* still resonates, his *War with the Newts* remains disturbingly relevant, and Čapek himself stands as a reminder that the best way to predict the future is to observe humanity and assume the worst, while hoping, naïvely, for the best.

His legacy is, in the end, a testament to the stubborn resilience of ideas. While his body succumbed to disease and his nation fell under occupation, his warnings lived on, forever unheeded, forever true, and forever awaiting the moment when someone, somewhere, will finally listen.

So. While Čapek certainly didn't *invent* robots, his *R.U.R.* is where the term comes from. Yet I hope you've found his story interesting and prophetic, because that was the entire point.

— **Further Reading** —

Bradbrook, Bohuslav, *Karel Čapek: In Pursuit of Truth, Tolerance, and Trust.* Sussex Academic Press, 1998.

Cepl, Petr, *Karel Čapek: Life and Work.* Artia, 1965.

---

[b] Examples include Boston Dynamics' *Atlas* robot, Honda's *ASIMO*, and MIT's *Cheetah*.

(Artist's conception)

Chapter 8 Phineas Gage

The Man Who Kept His Head (Mostly)

Phineas Gage's story is what happens when workplace safety regulations are merely a theoretical concept. It begins, as so many regrettable tales do, with a man, some explosives, and an iron rod. If you were wondering whether that combination led to anything good, the answer is a resounding "no."

In 1848, Gage was in Vermont, minding his own business and also minding several tons of railroad track, when an unexpected detonation transformed his skull into a high-speed transit system for a three-foot-long metal spike. The rod entered his head just below the left cheekbone, exited in a truly inconsiderate fashion through the top of his skull, and proceeded to land some distance away, no doubt feeling quite accomplished. The truly astonishing part? Gage not only survived, but according to witnesses, sat up and started talking, possibly wondering if he still had a job.

When Your Brain Decides to Improvise

So, other than losing any chances of being compared to Heathcliff, Franz Liszt, or George Clooney, his life continued, more or less as planned. It was only later that people realized Gage wasn't quite himself anymore. Before the accident, he was responsible, diligent, and generally the sort of person you'd trust with heavy machinery and explosives. Afterward, he developed the charming habit of swearing like a malfunctioning parrot, ignoring social norms, and displaying all the impulse control of a raccoon in a convenience store. His friends, in what might be the single greatest understatement in medical history, noted that he was "no longer Gage."

Today, we understand that the frontal lobe is the part of the brain responsible for keeping us from making spectacularly bad life choices. It's the reason most people don't yell at their bosses or attempt to pet wild bears. Gage's frontal lobe, unfortunately, had been forcibly evicted, and the result was a man whose personality now resembled that of a particularly unruly bar patron with one squinky eye.

A Remarkably Functional Disaster

Despite his, let's say, unconventional new approach to life, Gage didn't just sit around contemplating his newfound status as a medical curiosity. He moved to Chile and became a stagecoach driver, which raises several questions. Chief among them: Who thought this was a good idea? He was, after all, a man with demonstrably terrible impulse control and a recent history of traumatic brain injury, now entrusted with the responsibility of maneuvering large vehicles and dealing with the general public. And yet, by all accounts, he managed to do the job. This suggests that either (A) he retained more cognitive function than previously thought, or (B) 19th-century Chile had an exceptionally low bar for customer service. Keyboardist Chris Buzby, of the renowned progressive rock band Echolyn, formed an offshoot project called "Finneus Gauge" (yes, that's how they spelled it), an avant-rock fusion group. Buzby stated that he chose the name because their musical style was like that of Phineas Gage, with improvisation and (intentional) gaps in "musical memory."

Brains Are Weird, and So Is Fate

Gage eventually began suffering seizures, possibly a delayed consequence of the time his skull doubled as an artillery testing site, and died in 1860 at 36 years old. His skull, along with the infamous iron rod, was donated to science, where it remains on display at Harvard Medical School as a timeless testament to human resilience, neurological mystery, and what happens when physics decides to make an example out of someone.

His story continues to fascinate because it underscores something both profound and unsettling: who we are—our personalities, our temperaments, our carefully curated social facades—rests on a bundle of neurons that, under the wrong circumstances, can be rearranged like an unfortunate game of Jenga. Gage's case forced science to confront an uncomfortable truth: the soul, whatever that may be, is housed in a delicate, gelatinous mass that does not always behave as we expect.

And if you ever find yourself questioning that fact, just remember: somewhere in Harvard, a three-foot iron rod is still smirking.

— Further Reading —

Macmillan, Malcolm, *An Odd Kind of Fame: Stories of Phineas Gage*. MIT Press, 2000.

Chapter 9 Nikola Tesla: Overlooked Brilliance

Starry, Starry Mind

Nikola Tesla was, without question, one of history's great oddities: a genius so out of step with the world around him that it's a miracle we even know his name today. His innovations were so far ahead of their time, so surreal in their ambition, that to imagine they were conceived in the late 19th and early 20th centuries feels like recalling a fevered dream.

And yet, here we are, living in the very world that Tesla envisioned, unknowingly steeped in the genius of his unappreciated brilliance. Nikola Tesla's failures, though, are as fascinating as his triumphs, like a hero doomed to a tragic opera. In his version, the orchestra plays all the wrong notes.

If history's currents had been just a little less turbulent, Tesla might have been more than just a somewhat obscure character, a quirky figure whose inventions were either stolen, misunderstood, or abandoned entirely. The alternating current system we rely on today? It's his, a gift to humanity buried under the weight of corporate wars and underhanded tactics, not to mention the relentless campaign of one Thomas Edison. Edison, for all his talents, was something of a businessman with a personal vendetta: a vengeful inventor who wanted nothing more than to quash Tesla's better ideas, using the full might of his press machine to vilify him. Thomas Edison electrocuted an elephant in 1903 to try to show how dangerous Tesla's AC method was; because nothing screams "scientific integrity" like publicly executing an elephant in front of a crowd of gawking New Yorkers.[c] And Tesla, of course, was no match for such a campaign. He wasn't interested in the business of ideas; he was consumed with science and engineering. He had no time for corporate machinations or the cold logic of financial gain. He was, in some ways, too pure for his time: a person whose ideas floated above the petty squabbles of the world below. Imagine a man with visions of wireless electricity, global wireless communication, and technologies that seemed to spring from the realms of science fiction—and yet, the world he inhabited was much less interested in what he could offer than what they could take from him.

Tesla had struck a deal with George Westinghouse, a shrewd businessman who saw the potential of Tesla's alternating current system and was eager to back it. Tesla had secured a royalty agreement with Westinghouse worth millions in perpetuity. When Westinghouse Electric faced financial collapse, Tesla, out of loyalty or idealism, tore up the contract, forgoing what today would be worth tens of millions of dollars. He told George Westinghouse, "you don't have to pay me royalties." He had no desire to profit from his creation, so certain was he that the future of mankind was worth more than his own fortune.

But let's not forget that some of his most extraordinary ideas never saw the light of day; at least, not in the form he imagined them. His wireless transmission of energy, though an admirable dream, remained just that: a dream. As for his other outlandish ideas, they were buried under a pile of failures and lost opportunities. Yet in that, too, there's a kind of tragic genius: a man who saw the world not for what it was, but for what it *could be*.

Tesla, as he aged, wandered the streets of New York, penniless and largely ignored, a figure consumed by his own inventions, forgotten in his own time. And yet, if he had known, had he been able to glimpse the future, he might have seen his ideas take root, quietly changing

---

[c] Want to see this sadistic act? Edison filmed it. Just search YouTube or Dailymotion.

the world for good. It is an irony both absurd and inevitable that a man who lived in such struggle would leave behind a legacy that, in hindsight, feels like a secret whispered through time, like a forgotten radio transmission reverberating for decades after the broadcast ended.

In the end, Tesla was the kind of genius who didn't quite fit into the world of his own making: a man out of time, whose ideas became part of our everyday lives but whose personal story remains a little too strange, a little too tragic, and a little too inconvenient for the sanitized history books.

Some of Tesla's inventions, or improvements on earlier concepts:

1. Alternating Current (AC) System – a revolutionary method of electricity transmission that powers homes and industries today. Tesla's treatment of the concept made it commercially viable; it's what the world uses today.
2. Induction Motor – an electric motor that operates on alternating current, fundamental to modern electrical systems.
3. Tesla Coil – a high-voltage transformer used in wireless transmission experiments and scientific demonstrations.
4. Wireless Transmission of Energy – the concept of transmitting electricity without wires, which paved the way for later wireless technologies.
5. Radio (Radio Wave Transmission) – Tesla's early work in electromagnetic transmission laid the foundation for radio and arguably preceded the achievements of Guglielmo Marconi, who is often mistakenly credited as its sole inventor.
6. Rotary Magnetic Field – a key principle in AC motor design that revolutionized electric motor technology.
7. One-Way Valve ("Fluid Pump") – a valve system that used oscillating pressure instead of mechanical movement for fluid control.
8. Tesla Turbine – a bladeless turbine powered by smooth disks rather than blades, designed to generate energy.

9. Neon Lights – early development of neon lighting technology using electrical currents to excite gases, springboarding off the ideas of Georges Claude.
10. Oscillators – Tesla invented several types of oscillators.
11. Wardenclyffe Tower (Wireless Transmission Tower) – an unfinished project intended to provide global wireless communication and energy.
12. Tesla's Remote Control – the invention of the first remote-controlled boat using radio waves.
13. Tesla's Death Ray (Theoretical) – a proposed particle beam weapon, though it was never constructed or demonstrated.

— Further Reading —

Carlson, W. Bernard, *Tesla: Inventor of the Electrical Age*. Princeton University Press, 2013.

Seifer, Marc J., *Wizard: The Life and Times of Nikola Tesla*. Citadel Press, 1996.

Chapter 10 Somewhere, Over in Hollywoodland

A Nice Family Film, Poor Planning & Accidental Arson

The making of *The Wizard of Oz* was, in a word, catastrophic. In two words, hilariously catastrophic. You might think that a major Hollywood studio adapting a beloved children's book would involve some degree of order, but you would be mistaken. Instead, the production was basically a long experiment in human endurance, corporate negligence, and pyrotechnic miscalculations, all conducted under the assumption that the best way to make a great movie is to endanger as many people as possible.

Let's start with the script. MGM, in its infinite wisdom, decided that *The Wizard of Oz* needed to be rewritten approximately once every ten minutes. At least five writers had a go at it (humans, mind you, and not chimps), each one making drastic changes before passing it on like some sort of deranged literary relay race. The result was a screenplay that shifted tone unpredictably.

Then there was the casting, which went about as smoothly as "Impractical Joker" Sal Vulcano giving a wedding toast. Buddy Ebsen was the original Tin Man, until someone decided that painting his face with aluminum powder was a good idea. This, shockingly, turned out to be a very bad move, because it gave him a near-fatal case of metal poisoning. He was hospitalized, and simply replaced by Jack Haley, whose new, improved makeup merely caused persistent eye infections instead of full-body toxic shock, so, progress?

Judy Garland, meanwhile, was put through what we can only assume was a form of studio-sponsored hazing. Executives wanted the 16-year-old to look younger for some reason, so, to disguise her developing figure, they stuffed her into a corset so tight it could have doubled as structural support for a suspension bridge. Perhaps, though, they should've skipped the sexy ruby-red lipstick and just let her, you know, breathe? They also decided that the best way to keep her "fresh and energetic" was to feed her a steady diet of amphetamines and sleeping pills, presumably to ensure that she remained in a perfect state of either hyperactivity or unconsciousness at all times.

And then there was Margaret Hamilton, whose job as the Wicked Witch of the West required her to be repeatedly set on fire. During one scene, an effects mishap turned a dramatic exit into an unscheduled fireball. Not only did she suffer second-degree burns, but because the makeup on her face contained copper, her burns came with a bonus dose of toxic exposure. And yet, like a true professional, she came back to finish her scenes; though one imagines with significantly more wariness around Hollywood gaffers, "best boy electrics," and any open flames.

As if that weren't enough chaos, the movie burned through directors at a rate that suggested MGM was actively trying to set a world record. The production began with Richard Thorpe, who was immediately fired. George Cukor stepped in briefly before vanishing into the Hollywood ether. Victor Fleming took over and directed most of the film, only to be abruptly reassigned to *Gone with the Wind*, at which point King Vidor was brought in to sweep up the mess with a (metaphorical) burning broom. If this sounds like the studio had no idea what it was doing, that's because it absolutely did not.

Despite all of this—despite the script being rewritten on the fly, the makeup being actively toxic, and at least one cast member being literally engulfed in flames—the movie somehow turned out to be one of the most cherished films in cinematic history. So maybe there's a lesson in all of this: great art sometimes comes from chaos. Or, possibly, the lesson is "maybe don't light your actors on fire."

And if you're wondering about the "Hollywoodland" reference, Hollywood was originally known by that name. The famous sign was erected in 1923, and by the late 1940s, it had deteriorated. The "land" portion was simply removed.

— **Further Reading** —

Eyman, Scott, *Lion of Hollywood: The Life and Legend of Louis B. Mayer.*

Harmetz, Aljean, *The Making of The Wizard of Oz: Movie Magic and Studio Power in the Prime of MGM—and the Miracle of Production #1060.*

Chapter 11 What a Strange Trip It's Been

Affaire du Pain Maudit

The year was 1951. The war was over, everything was back to normal. And in the sleepy southern French town of Pont-Saint-Esprit next to the Rhône, something so sinister occurred almost too eerie for an apocalyptic thriller to contain.

Picture this: An entire town suddenly starts tripping so hard they see monsters, fire and all sorts of horrors that were not actually there. This was no government experiment gone wrong or the work of some shadowy plot. This was the dark side of ergot poisoning, a vile little fungus that likes to live in certain grains. I wasn't there in 1951 due to a medical condition called "not being born yet," but it hits close to me, as I live not too far from Pont St. Esprit and travel there on business and pleasure.

The incident is now called "l'affaire du pain maudit" - the Case of the Cursed Bread.

Ergot infects rye and other grains during flowering, replacing kernels with black, toxic sclerotia that can poison flour like some kind of party crasher. It turns out that ergot-tainted flour was available to the bakeries in the town. One baker in particular bought the tainted grain; every victim of the poisoning had bought bread from the Briand Bakery, considered the best *boulangerie* in Pont Saint Esprit. And when ergot decides to throw a party in your system, it doesn't settle for polite conversation and hors d'oeuvres; it's an all-out psychedelic storm, one that the village residents at the *"Bridge of the Holy Spirit"* were ill-prepared for.

The symptoms? A descent into delirium so complete that one man actually jumped into the Rhône River, convinced that his body was being devoured by snakes. Another, spurred by visions of fire and terror, leapt out of a window, presumably to experience the world from a new perspective. The streets of the town became a chaotic carnival of confusion, with people running around screaming, crying, and experiencing visions that would make a Salvador Dalí painting seem like a quixotic Renoir picnic scene. These people were, as we sometimes say, "tripping balls." But in French.

Meanwhile, the authorities, always keen to label things they don't understand as "mysterious," were scratching their heads, trying to figure out how an entire town could go absolutely bonkers. Eventually, the sinister truth came to light: the flour that Mssr. Briand had purchased was indeed contaminated with ergot, creating a kind of fungal cocktail that turned everyone's brain into a psychedelic funhouse mirror.

There seems to be no record of an apparition instructing someone to go to the Dagobah system to find Yoda, but think about how mind-blowing this is. People weren't just tripping out; they were tripping out *collectively*. One minute, they're going about their business, and the next, they're lost in a world of horrific visions that could only be rivaled by an industrial-sized bag of LSD, the stuff of medieval nightmares. Hunter S. Thompson and Jimi Hendrix could probably have handled it fine, but to the typical French townsperson who just wanted a hunk of bread with cheese on it, snakes and monsters and fire were quite the surprise.

It wasn't just about seeing apparitions, either; it was the complete breakdown of everything you think you know about reality. It's not like they signed up for a weekend in the desert with some questionable substances; no, they were victims of nature's mischief.

And then, to top it off, there's the ever-present whiff of conspiracy. Maybe it was something else. Later, mercury poisoning was suggested; fungicides too. Maybe something deeper, something that went beyond the simple, tragic folly of bad bread. One investigative journalist claimed it was due to CIA operations to test LSD.[3]

What we do know is that for a few days, over 250 people of Pont-Saint-Esprit experienced a kind of collective psychosis that'll go down in history as one of the weirdest, most bizarre moments of 20th-century French life. It resulted in at least five deaths; over 50 people were sent to psychiatric hospitals. It has been suggested, though contested, that similarly contaminated flour caused the hallucinations and paranoia that led to the witch trials Salem Witch Trials.[4]

"All I wanted was some bread..." I can hear some poor French woman lamenting.

— Further Reading —

Capron, Michel, *L'Affaire de Pont-Saint-Esprit: Une Enquête Inédite*.

DiSimone, Anthony, *The Devil's Bread: Ergotism and the Mass Poisoning at Pont-Saint-Esprit*.

Fullagar, Kate, *The Mass Poisoning at Pont-Saint-Esprit: Madness in a French Town*.

— Easy Viewing —
"The Cursed Bread Incident – Pont-Saint-Esprit 1951"
www.youtube.com/watch?v=xPJwpJpBNL4

Chapter 12 The War on Sparrows

Bye Bye Birdies

In 1958, the Chinese government, in what can only be described as one of history's greatest "Hold My Tsingtao" moments, decided that sparrows were an existential threat to agriculture and must be wiped off the face of the planet. This was part of the "Great Leap Forward" by Mao Zedong (literally, "mouse eats dung" in Chinese[d]), a program that, as it turns out, leaped mostly into disaster. The reasoning was simple: sparrows eat grain, and if you get rid of them, farmers will have more grain. If this logic seems suspiciously like something a five-year-old might come up with after a long day of licking lead paint, congratulations, you're already ahead of 1958 China.

Thus began the War on Sparrows, a campaign that mobilized an entire nation against small birds. People took to the streets with rifles, slingshots, and an enthusiasm usually reserved for the opening of an Apple Store. They shot sparrows out of the sky, destroyed nests, and, in a truly innovative display of nonsense, spent hours banging pots and pans to keep the birds flying until they dropped dead from sheer exhaustion. It was less an extermination effort and more an extended exercise in mass hysteria.

And, for a while, it worked! Sparrows died by the millions. Mao's officials, presumably high-fiving each other in a room filled with propaganda posters, declared victory. But then nature, in its classic passive-aggressive way, reminded humanity why tampering with the ecosystem is a bad idea. Without sparrows around to keep them in check, insects—especially locusts—flourished like never before. They swarmed the fields and devoured crops faster than an all-you-can-eat buffet during a football team's lunch break. The result? Widespread famine and starvation, proving once and for all that the

---

[d] Literally untrue.

only thing more dangerous than an unchecked locust swarm is an unchecked government plan based on terrible science.

Eventually, realizing they had declared war on the wrong species, officials abandoned the campaign. But the damage was done, and the War on Sparrows remains one of history's most baffling cautionary tales. If there's a moral to this story, it's probably something like: "Think before you eradicate an entire species," or maybe just, "Don't let dictators play ecologist."

— **Further Reading** —

Dikötter, Frank, *Mao's Great Famine: The History of China's Most Devastating Catastrophe, 1958–1962.*

Shapiro, Judith, *Mao's War Against Nature: Politics and the Environment in Revolutionary China.*

Chapter 13 The Tanganyika Laughter Epidemic

That's It! Everyone to Detention!

In 1962, an inexplicable and rather unsettling spectacle unraveled in what is now Tanzania. It started in a missionary school where some students began laughing their heads off, for no reason at all; not entirely unheard of in schools, which are no strangers to spontaneous outbreaks of dumb behavior. This time, however, it turned out to be something different. The laughter spread, like some sort of diabolical chain reaction, from one student to the next. Then it jumped the school walls and went rampaging through entire villages, mowing down innocent bystanders who suddenly found themselves laughing until they were too exhausted to move.

Authorities tried everything: medical intervention, quarantine, probably a few stern lectures, but nothing worked. People kept laughing. It got so bad that schools had to be shut down, not because of any reasonable, scientifically sound purpose but because nobody could get anything done when half the class was lying on the floor, convulsing with inexplicable hysteria.

Explanations were as varied as they were unsatisfying. Some called it "mass psychogenic illness," a fancy way of saying, "Well, that was just weird." Some said it was stress-related, with the political turbulence of the time so charged with anxiety that their nervous systems shorted out into laughter, a kind of crying, just less socially acceptable.

After several waves of hysteria over the course of more than a year, the epidemic fizzled out, presumably because people just got tired of laughing and had to go back to their normal lives. The whole incident remains one of history's most baffling cases of human absurdity; a reminder that, sometimes, the best science can do is throw up its hands and say, "Beats us!"

— Further Reading —

Bartholomew, Robert E., *Little Green Men, Meowing Nuns and Head-Hunting Panics: A Study of Mass Psychogenic Illness and Social Delusion.*

Hempelmann, Christian F., "The laughter of the 1962 Tanganyika 'laughter epidemic'." *HUMOR: International Journal of Humor Research.*

Chapter 14 The Luckiest Flight Attendant

Her Job Was to Serve Drinks, Not Defy Physics

Air travel, we are often assured, is the safest form of transportation, if one conveniently ignores the minor statistical footnote that, when something does go wrong, the odds of walking away are roughly equivalent to winning the lottery while being struck by lightning and attacked by a bear. Mid-air explosions, in particular, tend not to offer generous survival packages.

Yet, on January 26, 1972, Vesna Vulović took one of physics' rudest gestures—a free fall from 33,000 feet—and somehow turned it into an inconvenience rather than a death sentence. She had been working as a flight attendant on JAT Flight 367, a Yugoslav Airlines DC-9 that, thanks to what was widely believed to be a bomb, suddenly found itself less a plane and more a collection of rapidly descending debris over Czechoslovakia. The odds of survival? Theoretical, at best.

And yet, amid the metal confetti and the gravitational indifference of the universe, there was Vesna, plunging earthward in a wrecked section of fuselage, defying aerodynamics, medical textbooks, and common sense. What followed was the longest recorded free fall without a parachute, an accolade no sane person would ever actively attempt to claim.

Vulović's survival wasn't just a matter of blind luck, though luck certainly played a role. It was the kind of luck that suggests either divine intervention or that the cosmos occasionally enjoys a darkly comedic twist.

Premium Seating in the Disaster Section: Vesna had the dubious good fortune of being at the rear of the plane, which, in the bizarre physics of aviation catastrophes, meant she was in the most "survivable" section. It was as if fate had assigned her the first-class ticket for not dying.

A Crash Landing with Cushioning Perks: The wreckage, rather than smashing into something reliably lethal—say, a mountain or a parking lot—crashed into a snow-covered forest. The fuselage cradled Vesna in the same way an airbag cradles someone who has made several bad decisions in a row.

Sheer Stubborn Human Biology: Of course, she did not emerge unscathed. Her skull was fractured, her legs shattered, and her body an unfortunate case study in blunt force trauma. She spent days in a coma, presumably while her brain negotiated terms with reality. But against all odds, she came back, proving that the human body, while alarmingly fragile in everyday life, occasionally turns into a rubber ball when least expected.

The Aftermath: What To Do After Surviving the Impossible

Recovery was neither quick nor easy, but it was, by any reasonable standard, miraculous. Months in the hospital, a slow crawl back to mobility, and the kind of extensive surgery usually reserved for crash test dummies. She would walk again, though not without a limp; a permanent souvenir from her impromptu skydive.

Her post-fall existence became an odd mix of media sensation and bureaucratic absurdity. She returned to work with Yugoslav Airlines, though understandably, they kept her out of the air. The airline, perhaps realizing that she was now the world's most supernaturally unlucky—or lucky—flight attendant, reassigned her to desk duty, presumably to keep gravity from taking another shot at her.

Legacy: The Universe's Weird Sense of Humor

Vesna Vulović lived for decades beyond the day she should have died, outlasting the airline, the country that owned it, and most of the people who had somberly assumed her obituary would be written in 1972. She died in 2016 at the age of 66, having spent her life as a reluctant symbol of survival, luck, and the sheer unpredictability of existence.

Her story remains not just one of endurance, but of the fundamental strangeness of reality. Sometimes, the universe shrugs off the rules. Sometimes, fate deals you the worst possible hand and then, inexplicably, lets you keep playing.

And sometimes, when gravity decides to call, you just don't answer.

— Further Reading —

Graham, Ruth, *Slate*. "Bask in the Bracing Unsentimentality of Vesna Vulovic, the Only Person to Survive a 1972 Plane Crash." Dec 29, 2016. https://dub.sh/FPsDyTB

Chapter 15 The Convoy Craze

Got Your Ears On, Good Buddies?

So here's what happened: in 1975, a persona who went by the *nom de plume* "C.W. McCall" (basically a jingle writer who figured out how to make money by rhyming "smart" with "guard") unleashed a song called *"Convoy."* It told the heartwarming story of a bunch of truckers who used CB radios to organize the first known diesel-powered insurrection against The Man. And Americans, being who they are, heard this and went absolutely bonkers.[e]

Suddenly, people who used to get nosebleeds on escalators were slapping huge antennas on their Buicks and yelling things like "Break 1-9, got your ears on?" to nobody in particular. It was like someone turned down the fluoride in the water and everybody started cosplaying *Smokey and the Bandit* in real life.

Enter Radio Shack.

Now, Radio Shack had been this dusty little electronics store mostly frequented by guys who wore pocket protectors unironically. They sold things like diodes, mysterious knobs, and nine different types of wire that all did the same thing. But when *Convoy* hit, they found themselves at the center of a retail gold rush. The Shack was the only place in town where you could buy a CB radio without needing a government clearance or being an actual trucker. It was Christmas, Black Friday, and a tinfoil-hat ham radio convention all rolled into one.

People were buying CB radios like they thought the Soviets were going to invade through Cleveland. Stock in Tandy Corporation

---

[e] I don't think we can blame this one on bad bread.

(Radio Shack's corporate parent and, at the time, a sort of RadioShackopoly) *doubled*. Shareholders popped champagne. Radio Shack managers had to start locking the CBs behind glass like they were Fabergé eggs. (Or, in today's terms, just *eggs.*) At one point, CB radios accounted for over 20% of Radio Shack's sales.

Meanwhile, Hollywood, smelling diesel and money, jumped in with movies like *Breaker! Breaker*, *White Line Fever*, and eventually *Convoy*—a big-screen version of the song directed by Sam 'Blood Everywhere' Peckinpah—turned into CB propaganda reels. They featured trucks smashing through corrupt sheriff's blockades while love interests inexplicably appeared in the passenger seat wearing halter tops, delivering expositional dialogue at 80 mph.

Breaker breaker, we got an eye in the sky, back on the flip-flop.

As for the CB lingo? It was like someone took English, ran it through a wood chipper, and glued it back together with stale beer, a secret numbering system, and diesel fumes. "Bear in the air." "10-100." "Smokey's got a Kojak with a Kodak." It was beautiful gibberish, like Shakespeare in flannel. And the best part? Nobody knew what any of it meant, but *everybody pretended they did*, because that's how you bonded in the '70s: you faked it with confidence and a mustache. And maybe a leisure suit and platform shoes.

Then, like all good American frenzies—Pet Rocks, Crystal Pepsi, Sarah Palin—it ended. The airwaves got crowded, the FCC got cranky, and eventually the only people left using CBs were actual truckers and, possibly, your uncle Gary, who hasn't updated his technology since the Carter administration.

Radio Shack, for its part, cashed in and got out, like a grizzled prospector who struck gold, bought a boat, and quietly vanished. The CB boom became a strange, beautiful blip in the American timeline: a moment when everyone, from housewives in Nebraska to weird guys with raccoon caps in Georgia, believed they were part of a secret network, all because of a novelty country song and a bunch of men in eighteen-wheelers with names like "Rubber Duck" and "Pig Pen."

And honestly? It was glorious. Insane, but glorious, with a cringy sort of 1970s *bitchin' Camaro* face. If you'll pardon the anachronism.

— Further Reading —

Farman, Irvin, *Tandy's Money Machine: How Charles Tandy Built Radio Shack into the World's Largest Electronics Chain*.

Loftesness, Scott, "The Rise and Decline of CB Radio." *Scott Loftesness Blog*, November 12, 2023. https://sjl.us/2023/11/12/the-rise-and-decline-of-cb-radio/

Chapter 16 The Vampire of Sacramento

Bloodbath and Beyond

Look, most of us have, at some point, stared into the abyss of our bathroom fixtures and wondered if they might have something profound to say. Like, perhaps, that your morning routine is a travesty or that your soap dish is sick of holding the same melting sliver of Irish Spring from 1994. But Richard Trenton Chase? He took the concept of "hearing voices" and, rather than seek professional help like a sensible lunatic, decided household items like his soap dish and fridge were licensed hematologists issuing urgent medical advice. Oh, and he feared abduction by Nazi UFOs. But then, don't we all.

According to Chase, the problem was that his blood was drying up. Now, when faced with such a concern, an ordinary person might, at the very least, consider consulting *a doctor*. But Chase, who could generously be described as "someone who made bad choices," went a different route. The *only* way to keep his blood from turning into strawberry Quik powder, he decided, was to drink other people's blood. Not eat a hamburger, not take an iron supplement, not *literally anything else*, just to straight-up Nosferatu his way through Sacramento.

So, in late 1977, Chase embarked on what can be described as a one-man reenactment of every horror movie ever banned in Sweden. He began with small animals, blending their organs into smoothies like some kind of deeply confused paleo influencer. Then, evidently deciding this wasn't quite *psychotic enough*, he escalated to home invasion, mass murder, and possibly the worst remodeling work any California home has ever suffered. A man who was in desperate need of a lobotomy instead performed amateur phlebotomies.

Chase didn't just kill people. He *ruined* crime scene investigators' careers. His rampage was so appallingly grotesque that even seasoned cops walked into his crime scenes and thought, *You know what? I think I'll go sell insurance instead.* By the time the police caught him, Chase was sitting in his apartment, absolutely marinated in evidence, looking as confused as if he had just been asked to explain compound interest. By comparison, Jeffrey Dahmer had standards.

At trial, his legal defense was essentially a shrug and the faint hope that the jury might be open to the argument, *"Well, Your Honor, his soap dish said so."* Unfortunately for him, neither the jury nor the judge found "the bathroom accessories made me do it" particularly convincing. Taking advice from a dog or a Ouija board makes a *little* more sense. Soap dish? Nope, *that* is crazy.

He was sentenced to death, but in a twist of fate that should surprise absolutely no one, Chase somehow managed to take himself out before the state could. In 1980, he overdosed on his prison medication, which suggests that even his *exit strategy* was an unsettling mix of poor planning and baffling commitment.

And so ended the life of the Vampire of Sacramento, one of the few serial killers whose crimes are so outrageous they seem *less* plausible the more you hear about them. The lesson here? If your soap dish starts giving you life advice, maybe, just maybe, don't listen. Same if your refrigerator starts talking back.

— Further Reading —

Schechter, Harold, *The Serial Killer Files: The Who, What, Where, How, and Why of the World's Most Terrifying Murderers*. Ballantine Books, 2003.

Chapter 17 Liquid Gold

The Canadian Job

If you ever needed proof that Canada is a nation trapped in a charming but deeply absurd contradiction, consider this: it has a *strategic maple syrup reserve*. This is not satire. It exists, a vast stockpile of viscous, caramel-colored nectar, governed with the iron fist of a Soviet-era planning committee. The Federation of Quebec Maple Syrup Producers (FPAQ), a name as comically innocuous as it is insidiously bureaucratic, controls the trade with the severity of a petro-state autocracy. The only difference between the FPAQ and OPEC is that OPEC doesn't force its members to stockpile barrels of crude oil under lock and key like they're housing nuclear warheads.

But Canada, being a nation that combines an almost aggressive politeness with a deep-seated commitment to statist meddling, has ensured that maple syrup, of all things, remains a commodity so tightly regulated that it was only a matter of time before a group of enterprising criminals saw an opportunity. And so, between 2011 and 2012, a band of thieves executed a heist so spectacularly Canadian that it belongs in a museum dedicated to the nation's quirks.

Their crime? Stealing *18 million dollars' worth of syrup*. Not money. Not gold. *Syrup*.

How did they do it? Not through violent means, nor with anything so cinematic as an underground tunnel or an elaborate system of security bypasses. Or a fleet of candy-apple Mini Coopers. No, they simply *rented a warehouse*, used trucks to transport syrup from an FPAQ facility, siphoned the syrup, replaced the contents with water and returned the trucks like nothing had happened. The stolen syrup was then sold to legitimate distributors. In any other country, this kind of brazen theft would have been stopped by, say, a rudimentary inventory system. But in the Kafkaesque world of Quebec's maple bureaucracy, it took *months* before someone noticed anything.

The heist, of course, prompted a sweeping investigation—one that involved both the Canadian authorities and the FPAQ's own Syrup Police, a phrase so preposterous it hardly needs embellishment. Eventually, the perpetrators were caught, prosecuted, and sentenced, proving that Canada may tolerate many things: long-winded government intervention, oppressive dairy quotas, Celine Dion; but it will *not* stand for unregulated syrup.

And here lies the lesson: when a commodity is artificially inflated in price and controlled with an iron fist, the inevitable response is black-market defiance. Quebec's syrup cartel, like all cartels, creates criminals by design. What happened here was not merely a heist—it was an economic inevitability. And that, perhaps, is the most ridiculous thing of all.

— Further Reading —
Gendron, Josée, *La grande escroquerie du sirop d'érable*. Les Éditions La Presse, 2013.

Strategic Maple Syrup Reserve (artist's conception)

Chapter 18 Mark Wahlberg and 9/11

Almost Departed

The odds against Mark Wahlberg's survival on September 11, 2001, were astronomical; except, of course, they weren't. His absence from American Airlines Flight 11 was not a miracle or a premonition but an instance of the everyday chaos that governs human schedules. A last-minute change of plans saved his life, and in the ledger of history's near-misses, this was an especially dramatic one.

Now, Wahlberg has made no secret of his feelings about that day. He has, at times, spoken about it with gratitude and, at others, with the kind of hypothetical confidence that only hindsight affords. He once speculated that, had he been on the plane, things might have played out differently. This is akin to imagining oneself out-maneuvering history's most irreversible moments. The truth is that hijackings are chaotic, terrifying, and exceedingly difficult to thwart without prior knowledge, specialized training, or, preferably, a complete absence of knife-wielding terrorists.

Still, Wahlberg's experience captures something universal: the eerie realization that life's most profound events often turn on the tiniest of pivots. A missed bus, a delayed flight, a casual change in itinerary: these are the mundane mechanisms by which people escape disaster or, in many tragic cases, stumble directly into it. In the grand statistical churn of human fate, Wahlberg's survival was neither fated nor foreseen, but simply another reminder that history's gears turn.

You'll recall that Wahlberg starred in Seth MacFarlane's film *Ted*. Coincidentally, MacFarlane was also scheduled for Flight 11, but due to a hangover after an evening of celebrations on September 10, he missed the flight.[5] Sometimes, missing a flight isn't luck or destiny. It's just life, throwing darts in the dark.

Chapter 19 Daniel Tammet

A Synesthetic Prodigy

If you were to engineer a human being specifically to make everyone else feel inadequate, you might end up with something like Daniel Tammet. He recites Pi to tens of thousands of decimal places, learns entire languages before most people can figure out a foreign metro system, and experiences numbers as if they were living, breathing entities, while the rest of us struggle to calculate a restaurant tip.

He is, in essence, what would happen if a quantum computer developed a sense of humor and an unusually well-adjusted personality.

A Brain That Shouldn't Work But Somehow Does

Tammet's childhood was a mess of neurological chaos: epileptic seizures, relentless crying, and an overall sense that his brain was operating on a different frequency from everyone else's. While most babies spend their early years mastering the high art of not falling over, he seemed preoccupied with something much larger, as if he were busy decrypting the finer details of the cosmos while his parents just wished he'd take a nap.

And then, instead of leading to disaster, his unusual neurological cross-wiring resulted in an intellectual superpower. He began experiencing numbers in a way that would make Pythagoras weep with envy. Each digit was not just a symbol but an entity, complete with color, texture, lights, and emotion. If you or I look at the number 289, we see, well, *289*. Tammet sees a luminous shape, possibly shimmering, possibly slightly annoyed. His mind is a living art gallery of arithmetic, where prime numbers in particular stand out like grand masterpieces and ordinary calculations unfold like Shakespearean drama.

Conversely, walking through a big city conjures images in Daniel's mind of floating numbers that sparkle, cascade, and superimpose themselves on the streets and buildings. A skyscraper? Daniel's brain sees it as an imposing blue "9." In his book *Born on a Blue Day*, he calls nine "the most troublesome" number: large, tall, and intimidating, evoking feelings of anxiety and concern. Damn those nines!

Languages? No Problem.

As if his mathematical prowess weren't enough, Tammet also treats languages like particularly enjoyable crossword puzzles. Most people attempting to learn Icelandic—a language that sounds like someone gargling rocks while reciting a legal document—would quickly give up and order a beer in English instead. Tammet, however, enough Icelandic in a single week to hold a live interview on Icelandic television. A *week*. The average person takes longer to figure out the remote control for a new television.

This is a man who doesn't just acquire information: he devours it, metabolizes it, and then somehow turns it into something even more remarkable. In *Born on a Blue Day*, he doesn't just recount his abilities; it offers a rare glimpse into the mind of someone who lives at the intersection of logic and poetry, where numbers have character and words have weight beyond their dictionary definitions.

The Cosmic Joke of Intelligence

There's a certain irony to Tammet's existence, one that would be deeply amusing if it weren't also a little unsettling: his extraordinary mind, so seemingly well-calibrated for understanding the universe, was forged in the unpredictable fires of neurological disorder. Had his brain developed in a way considered "normal," he might have been just another person slogging through tax forms and wondering why Excel won't do what he wants. Instead, the apparent misfire of his early years set off a chain reaction that produced one of the most extraordinary minds of our time.

And that raises an uncomfortable thought: how many other geniuses, their potential locked away by biology, fate, or sheer bad luck, never get their chance?

Tammet was fortunate, if one can call neurological turbulence a form of luck. But his story is more than just an account of intelligence and perception gone supernova; it's a reminder that the brain, in all its mysterious and occasionally malfunctioning wonder, is both the most fragile and the most formidable thing in the known universe.

And if you need proof, just ask Tammet. In Icelandic. Or Estonian, or Finnish, or French, or German, or Lithuanian... He'll have an answer.

To watch an absolutely riveting documentary about him, just search your favorite video site for "Daniel Tammet the boy with the incredible brain."

— Further Reading —

Tammet, Daniel, *Born on a Blue Day: Inside the Extraordinary Mind of an Autistic Savant*. Free Press, 2007.

Treffert, Darold A., *Islands of Genius: The Bountiful Mind of the Autistic, Acquired, and Sudden Savant*. Jessica Kingsley Publishers, 2010.

Hermelin, Beate., *Bright Splinters of the Mind: A Personal Story of Research with Autistic Savants*. Jessica Kingsley Publishers, 2001.

Chapter 20 Operation Paul Bunyan

The Most Overkill Landscaping Job in History

Most people, when confronted with an inconvenient tree, consult an arborist. Maybe they borrow a chainsaw. What they don't do, typically, is summon an armada of warplanes, an infantry division, and enough firepower to overthrow a small government. But then again, most people aren't dealing with North Korea, where logic takes a backseat to cult-of-personality tantrums, and where even inanimate objects seem to require ideological vetting.

Our story begins in the Joint Security Area (JSA), a place so tense that blinking too aggressively might qualify as an act of war. Here stood a poplar tree, a leafy obstruction blocking the view between U.S. and South Korean outposts. In a normal country, this would be the sort of issue resolved by a park ranger with a branch clipper. But this was the DMZ, where even the grass probably had an intelligence file.

So, on August 18, 1976, a team of U.S. and South Korean soldiers arrived with axes to do what should have been the least controversial act in the history of military operations: pruning a tree. Unfortunately, North Korea, never one to miss an opportunity for cartoon villainy, decided this was an act of imperialist aggression. A group of North Korean soldiers ambushed them, and in a scene that would have been comically medieval if it weren't so grotesque, hacked two U.S. officers to death with axes and clubs. Because nothing says "glorious revolutionary struggle" quite like bludgeoning unarmed men over a landscaping dispute.

North Korea, presumably expecting another round of strongly worded letters and diplomatic hand-wringing, was in for a rather shocking surprise.

Three days later, in a masterstroke of overkill, the U.S. launched Operation Paul Bunyan: a response so theatrically excessive that it makes most action movies look like understated realism. Hundreds of troops, backed by tanks, attack helicopters, and strategic bombers, assembled at the DMZ. Navy warships loomed offshore. A fleet of B-52s—the kind that typically precede nuclear annihilation—flew in visible range of Pyongyang. And at the center of all this might, all this hardware, all this absurd firepower... was a team of lumberjacks.

Yes. Lumberjacks. U.S. military engineers with chainsaws and axes.

The U.S. wasn't here to fight a war. It was here to prove that it could. If it wanted to. At any time. Against anyone. Even, or especially, over a tree.

And so, under the watchful eye of the most excessive security detail in landscaping history, the tree was unceremoniously chainsawed into oblivion. It was a meticulously choreographed display of nonchalant dominance, a scene so ridiculous and yet so effective that North Korea, usually the undisputed global champion of ridiculous overreaction, did something entirely out of character: it backed down. Kim Il Sung issued a vague statement of regret, which was as close to an apology as the regime had ever given or likely ever will. Hawkeye Pierce would have hated this.

Thus, Operation Paul Bunyan entered the annals of history as an almost surreal case study in power projection. It remains a lesson in deterrence, diplomacy, and the fine art of making a point without having to fire a shot. And somewhere, in the grand cosmic record of human absurdities, there is an entry about the time an empire flexed its military muscle: not to claim land, not to overthrow a dictator, not even to seize resources, but to prove a point with a chainsaw.

Because sometimes, in the strange and perplexing theater of geopolitics, the best way to avoid war is to show, in no uncertain terms, just how easily you could win one.[6]

Chapter 21 The Würzburg Witch

You Got Your Spell on Me, Baby

"I read a book on the Salem Witch Trials," declared Dinesh D'Souza in a 2011 speech, "...I had been educated to believe the Salem Witch Trials had killed thousands, or at the very least hundreds of people. I discovered that the number of people executed was, in fact... *eighteen*."[f] He seems completely unaware that Salem wasn't the only place where people killed "witches."

Fade out, fade in, 1746, Würzburg, Germany—just another sleepy, charming German town, right? Wrong. In this little slice of Bavarian history, a bunch of nuns suddenly started to behave like the last season of a reality TV show no one asked for. They were screaming. They were convulsing. And not in the normal, "oh, I stubbed my toe" way. No, they were writhing, twitching, and falling into some serious trance-like states, so much so that you'd think they'd accidentally taken a double dose of something you'd never expect to find in a nun's medicine cabinet. The whole thing was so out of control; people were forced to wonder if they were experiencing divine intervention or, more likely, the early stages of a spontaneous group mental breakdown.

Naturally, the town wasn't about to let a good opportunity for a public spectacle go to waste. They had their theories, ranging from the sensible (bad cheese) to the utterly absurd (the Devil himself was, apparently, up for a visit). But, because every good story needs a villain, the blame was swiftly pinned on a local elderly woman, Maria Renata Singer von Mossau: because, why not? If you're looking for a scapegoat in 18th-century Europe, a "witch" is about as good a bet as any.

And so, in what seems to have been a clear case of mass hysteria—or again, possibly just fungus-infected bread as testified earlier in

---

[f] www.youtube.com/watch?v=ZyTCngojsI8&t=690s accessed 23 April 2025.

Pont St. Esprit—the woman was accused, tried, and executed in 1749. The spectacle, though, was nothing compared to the extended outcome: a town so mired in superstition and dread, it made the Salem witch trials look like a light-hearted comedy special. But, in the end, it wasn't the Devil's handiwork. It was just people doing what they always do when faced with things they can't explain: panic, persecute, and then... turn it into a public execution. Very 18th century.

So, listening to Dinesh D'Souza's 2011 speech, we learn it was not just the eighteen at Salem, but in fact, one more, *nineteen witches*?

Right. And the *Titanic* had a "small leak." Würzburg didn't just dabble in witch hunts, it treated them like an enthusiastic amateur baker who just got their first stand mixer. In the earlier "witch trials" in the town from 1625 to 1631, over 600 executions took place, each one delivered with the solemnity of a church picnic and the logistics of a medium-sized war. People were strangled, interrogated, burned alive, and accused of flying through keyholes on brooms, which, as you might expect, was a rare skill even back then. There was a sense of *vigorous creativity* to the charges: everything from making milk curdle to "causing a bishop's gout to flare up suspiciously."

So, over a century later, Maria Renata was just the closing act in a theater of the grotesque that had been playing to sold-out crowds for decades. Her case had it all: demonic possession, wild nun choreography, and the sort of courtroom drama that makes *Law & Order: Heresy Victims Unit* sound plausible. But by then, Würzburg was basically running a franchise. The pyres weren't just symbolic; they were recurring expenses in the town budget. You can imagine the monthly town hall meetings: "Any new witches this quarter?" "Yes, plus a widow who owns three cats and brews a suspiciously good broth."

And sure, you could blame it all on the era, on superstition, fear, and poor access to Netflix; but that only gets you so far. Europe had a talent for this sort of thing.[g] Hundreds of thousands of innocent Cathars got steamrolled centuries earlier, thanks to a pope who decided that spiritual ambiguity was best solved by an extended military campaign.[7][8] ("Kill them all; God will know His own" was not exactly an HR-approved motto.) Then there's Pope Gregory IX's crusade against the "witches" of Stedingen, Germany, resulting in some 30,000 innocent people killed.[9][10][11] Across the continent, witch hunting was less about theology and more about civic planning with a touch of arson.

If history teaches us anything, besides never to trust "traders" in the 17th century if you have darkish skin, it's that the combination of unchecked authority and a vaguely defined enemy can lead to *some really awkward town festivals*. Würzburg's bonfires weren't just tragedies; they were warnings, screaming across centuries: *Beware the pious when they start taking attendance.*

— Further Reading —

Behringer, Wolfgang, *Witchcraft Persecutions in Bavaria: Popular Magic, Religious Zealotry, and Reason of State in Early Modern Europe*. Cambridge University Press, 1997.

---

[g] And don't forget the Bible, "Thou shalt not suffer a witch to live" (Ex 22:18).

Chapter 22 Driving While Wealthy

...And Other Tales of Law and Disorder.

Switzerland v. Ferrari

Fines for traffic violations in Switzerland are calculated based on income and wealth. In 2010, Swiss courts issued what's believed to be the world's largest speeding fine: 1 million Swiss francs (about $1.1 million) to a Swedish driver caught doing 290 km/h (180 mph) in a Ferrari.[12] If Enzo were still around, at least *he* would be proud.

And Finland Too

Like Switzerland, traffic fines in Finland are calculated based on the offender's income. In 2015, Finnish businessman Reima Kuisla was caught doing a mere km/h (14 mph) over the limit, and was fined €54,000, thanks to his annual income of €6.5 million. How would they know? Well, the authorities accessed his 2013 tax return.[13] On Facebook he posted "Finland is impossible to live in for certain kinds of people who have high incomes and wealth." The poor oppressed man!

In 2002, an executive at Nokia was hit with a 116,000 euro fine for speeding on his Harley Davidson in Finland. His penalty was based on a salary of €14 million.

Animal Farce

But things used to be... simpler? In medieval Europe, animals could be brought to trial for crimes. In 1457, a sow and her piglets were tried in Savigny, France for murdering a child, although no murder weapon was found, and neither did the prosecution prove any motive.[14] The porcine perp was found guilty and executed, but her piglets were acquitted due to their youth and "corrupting influence of their mother."

Salt of the Town

The town of Venice, Italy once declared war on the neighboring city of Chioggia because Chioggia's salt production competed with Venice's salt monopoly. This is one of many "salt wars" throughout history where cities literally fought over salt rights.

Salt was incredibly valuable in the ancient world as a preservative and nutrient. In fact, Roman soldiers were given a salt allowance called "salarium," the root of our modern word "salary."

The Scarlet Vest

In Singapore, littering fines escalate dramatically for repeat offenders. A third-time offender can be fined up to $10,000 and required to perform public cleaning while wearing a bright vest publicly branding them as a litterer.

In Death Shall You Not Part

In Svalbard, Norway, it's essentially illegal to die. The Arctic climate prevents bodies from decomposing, so terminally ill residents must relocate to mainland Norway. Yet bodies buried there for nearly a century still contain perfectly preserved smallpox samples.

Chapter 23 Karen in the House

"I'm calling corporate. I'll get you fired for this!"

The "Karen" phenomenon—which I'm legally obligated to inform you is NOT named after any specific Karen, so if your name happens to be Karen, please don't hunt me down in the parking lot demanding my supervisor's contact information—represents humanity's most perfect achievement in cataloging suburban terror since we invented homeowner associations.

The French have a verb for this: "raler." It's more than just "se plaindre" (to complain). It means *to complain about everything* and be satisfied with nothing, always grumbling. But face it, the Karen does much more than just grumble. That's why we see videos titled "Disturbed Karen," "Entitled Karen" and "Karen freakout."

Picture this: You're seventeen, earning $7.25 an hour folding sweaters at the mall, when suddenly the air pressure drops. Cash registers freeze. Small children instinctively seek shelter. Through the automatic doors strides a woman whose SUV almost certainly sports a bumper sticker that reads "My pronouns are: TRY/ME," and a suspiciously self-satisfied aura, like she's just returned from a workshop on weaponized righteousness. Her highlights have highlights. Her nails could puncture spacecraft. Her sunglasses, emblazoned with a brand name so oversized you'd think it was a billboard, practically shout their price tag stronger than their ability to block the sun.

YouTubers gleefully bestow them with fittingly mocking sobriquets: *Mall Karen*, *Swimming Pool Karen*, *Skatepark Karen*, *Beach Karen*, and countless other location-specific titles, each more satisfying than the last. In fairness to the sexes, there's no shortage of "male Karen" videos circulating out there; but that is a whole other can of blowhards for another time.

Karen is ready to pop. Something's wrong—catastrophically wrong—with her food order, or service, or existence. And she's determined to karensplain her discontent to anyone within earshot, while ignoring shouts of *shut up, Karen!* from annoyed bystanders.

DEFCON 1.

The Karen doesn't merely complain; she unleashes a symphony of indignation that Bach would envy. Short, staccato demands ("Where. Is. Your. Manager?") followed by sprawling, run-on manifestos detailing her customer journey with the meticulousness of someone documenting war crimes for The Hague. This syntactical rollercoaster is her trademark. Lay a hand on a Karen? "You're literally raping me!" she may claim. Karen *loves* the word "literally" but she doesn't know what it means. Literally.

If she discovers someone committing the act of SWB at a hotel,[h] she'll demand to see a room key to prove they're guests, and call the cops for backup. She's irate at those who dare infringe on her delusion: furious, yet somehow untouchable, convinced she is immune to consequence, and above all rules and laws. What elevates the Karen beyond garden-variety complainers is her magnificent relationship with reality, which can best be described as "open to interpretation" or "more of a serving suggestion, really." Facts orbit her grievances like anxious moons, never quite making contact. Store policy stated "no returns after 30 days"? That sign obviously wasn't meant for *her*. The restaurant closed at 9:00? Her watch, and presumably the entire space-time continuum, disagrees.

The truly transcendent Karen—the Karen Emeritus—wields the phone call to authorities as casually as others might use a butter knife. Somewhere in America right now, a 911 dispatcher is listening to a woman report the federal crime of "a Hispanic-looking person suspiciously near my Pilates studio." Police arrive to find themselves transformed into customer service representatives with guns, medi-

---

[h] "Swimming While Brown."

ating disputes about pool access or improper waste bin placement with the gravity normally reserved for hostage negotiations.

When arrested, Karen either dissolves into a shrieking toddler demanding apple juice and her constitutional rights, or she starts planning her new life as a wealthy civil-rights martyr-slash-Instagram-influencer with a lawsuit that will "literally bankrupt the entire police department" as she *demands* names and badge numbers, while also shouting "No. I am NOT under arrest!" and "Do you know who I am? *I make more money than all of you put together!*"

The Karen's natural habitat stretches from Starbuck's to Pottery Barn, but she excels in anywhere others are enjoying themselves. Parks, concerts, and restaurants become staging grounds for her one-woman crusade against unauthorized happiness.

Her power moves include filming confrontations on a phone held at the exact angle to make her look most victimized, despite being the only person speaking. Her other arm is outstretched in the direction of her victim, with index finger raised. She wears a combination of a hateful sneer and self-satisfied smile.

What makes this self-anointed marvel truly fascinating is how she manages to occupy contradictory states simultaneously. She demands respect while offering none; invokes rules while breaking them; seeks protection from authorities she simultaneously dismisses; and—in a feat of cognitive gymnastics that would impress Simone Biles—positions herself as both oppressor and oppressed depending on which role offers tactical advantage in the moment.

The Karen isn't merely asking for the manager. She's demanding to speak to the universe about its failure to revolve exclusively around her axis, and she's brought the receipts to prove her case.

Chapter 24 The Strandbeest

Beach Blanket Bots

Nothing reminds you of humanity's misplaced priorities quite like watching a ten-legged, wind-powered contraption march confidently down a Dutch shoreline while somewhere in the world, a perfectly good subway system is falling apart. Theo Jansen, a man with the soul of a Renaissance artist and the patience of a lunatic, has spent decades ensuring that these skeletal aberrations—equal parts Da Vinci sketch and insectoid fever dream—don't just exist, but thrive.

And thrive they do. Powered by nothing but the hubris of the wind, these PVC-spined creatures don't merely move; they strut. They clatter along the sand in an unsettlingly lifelike procession, as if some giant, misguided deity had attempted to reinvent the centipede and then given up halfway. Their mechanics are a study in sheer, beautiful overcomplication: Jansen has essentially spent thirty years proving that, yes, you can build a walking machine that requires no engines, no electronics, and absolutely no excuse to exist other than "Why the hell not?"

Thanks to Jansen, these things are evolving in a way that suggests they might one day start unionizing. Some can detect water and back away. Others anchor themselves to the beach when storms approach, demonstrating better survival instincts than certain politicians. They are also strangely familiar, despite their eerie, otherworldly appearance. Watching a Strandbeest march down the beach is like watching a stiff creature from Fellini on stilts: a graceful, awkward, unnecessary parade of motion.

So where can one see these mad, wonderful machines in their natural habitat? For Dutch beaches, head to Scheveningen or Kijkduin, where Jansen lets his Strandbeests roam free like some mad zookeeper who traded *Jurassic Park* for PVC dinosaurs. They occasionally also appear in international exhibitions; and you might just spot one awkwardly schlepping through a museum or an art festival reminding us all that the world is at its best when it is a little ridiculous.

— **Further Reading** —

Jansen, Theo, *Strandbeest: The Dream Machines of Theo Jansen*. Taschen, 2016.

Ballard, J. G., *The Wind as a Tool: Theo Jansen's Strandbeest Project*. MIT Press, 2017.

A strandbeest, exhibited on the Linz city square during Ars Electronica, 2005

Part 2 - Humans vs. Engineering

For a species that never misses an opportunity to declare itself the apex of intelligence, we have an uncanny talent for engineering our own fiascos. One might assume that after several thousand years of trial, error, and the occasional city-evaporating miscalculation, we'd have developed an instinct for, say, not constructing bridges that interpret a light breeze as an existential crisis or strapping skyscraper-grade explosives to vehicles primarily designed to transport people. And yet, against all odds, here we are.

Progress, as it turns out, has the impulse control of a caffeinated toddler. What follows is an exploration of those moments when human ingenuity collided headfirst with human oversight—often at high velocity. These are tales of boardrooms where confident men in expensive suits assured everyone that what worked in a PowerPoint slide would surely work in reality. They are case studies in what happens when ambition outpaces caution and when the laws of physics, unimpressed by our optimism, decline to offer a refund.

We have buildings that collapsed because no one stopped to ask whether the ground underneath them was, in fact, optional. We have marvels of mechanical engineering undone by an oversight so basic that a particularly astute houseplant might have spotted it. And we have visionary projects that transformed from triumph to tragedy at roughly the speed of a stock market crash, all presided over by people who found it easier to approve budgets than to mention that perhaps launching untested machinery with actual humans inside was less of a "bold strategy" and more of a "felony waiting to happen."

Yet, amid the flaming wreckage of our most audacious blunders, there remains something undeniably human: a mix of genius, recklessness, and the absolute certainty that, this time, we've got it right. The universe does not award participation trophies, but if it did, we'd be drowning in them. These failures, however spectacular, are merely the cost of our relentless drive to tinker, improve, and hurl ourselves into the unknown with the conviction of a gambler on a losing streak. And history suggests we will continue paying that price: willingly, repeatedly, and with an enthusiasm that is equal parts admirable and deeply concerning.

Chapter 25 The Erfurt Latrine Disaster

Slip Slidin' Away

It was in July, during a sweltering summer of 1184, a mere 840 or so years ago, when feudal politics of the Holy Roman Empire were at their fiercest, and the castle of Erfurt became the venue for a tragedy so absurd and grotesque that it would resonate far into history, leaving behind not glories but rather a monument to the frailty of power. The great hall, with history itself creaking underfoot on timber, was filled with nobles and knights, each created by consummate art to stand as a symbol of authority; each one a guardian of a world where rank meant everything, bloodlines all.

Called by King Henry VI, a son of Emperor Frederick Barbarossa, these men robed in silks, chains of mail, and armory engraved with lineage came to mediate a dispute between the Landgrave of Thuringia, Ludwig III, and Archbishop Konrad of Mainz. The weight of this gathering did not escape anyone present: the flickering torchlight barely illuminated the ghastly arguments. The air reverberated with tension, fueled by resentments and power plays, squeezing the contours of their fate, while the elites squabbled destinies against one another within the hall. Yet no one amongst them ever dreamed of the final, unspeakable turn of their fates.

Men Against The Pee

Then came the sound, a splintering, calamitous crack followed by the thunderous, ungodly collapse of the very floor beneath them. What followed was not simply the fall of stone and timber; it was a deeper, more primordial fall into chaos and degradation.

The floor gave way.

Those noblemen, self-adorned in their finest garb, the very symbols of human achievement, plummeted downward, not into death by sword or plague, but into the bowels of the castle's latrine pit. Below, the cesspool—a grotesque abyss of human waste—

waited to swallow them whole. They did not fall into stone or soil, but into a suffocating, putrid mire. The stench alone was enough to twist the soul.

The hall erupted into wild panic. Those encased in heavy armor sank almost immediately, with the sheer weight of their gilded regalia pulling them into the festering depths of fecal filth. Others screamed for help, flailing in utter desperation, their cries swallowed by the suffocating embrace of excrement. Those who managed to cling to any semblance of debris or broken timber were pulled gasping and retching from the pit, their dignity completely gone, their bodies sullied with the shame of the cesspool. Many others, dozens of men of high lineage, perished, drowning not in blood but in their own refuse. And all, without paddle amongst them (not that it would have helped).

Above, those fortunate enough to escape the fall recoiled in horror and disbelief. King Henry VI, untouched by the disaster, gazed down at the scene with the detached glance of one who had seen power reduced to its most humiliating form. What transpired below was not typical military death, by blade; nor typical middle-ages death by plague, but a brutal annihilation of pride, swallowed whole by the very filth these men had long sought to control.

As the chaos ebbed and those who could be saved were pulled from the pit shivering and vomitous, the damage was tallied. The great hall, once the stage for lofty negotiations and aristocratic airs, now reeked of death, of degradation, of a cruel irony that no one, least of all those who had been present, could have predicted. What had been a gathering of men who viewed themselves as the very architects of fate was now reduced to a grotesque (and smelly) farce.

The Erfurt Latrine Disaster was not just a moment in medieval history; it became a ghastly reminder—among many others—that, after all, nothing in this world is more fragile than the edifice of human pride.

While wars, betrayals, and pestilences are celebrated through history, very few incidents epitomize the sheer absurdity of human ambition like this tragedy, where even the loftiest of nobles descended into a putrid abyss and were engulfed by their own follies, their power and prestige rapidly extinguished by the very filth they previously sought to control.[15][16]

Chapter 26 The Vasa Ship Disaster

Top-Heavy, Overloaded, and Doomed

On a crisp summer afternoon in 1628, Sweden's most ambitious warship, the *Vasa*, sailed forth from Stockholm's harbor. With towering masts and lavish carvings, she struck an imposing figure—an ornate thunderhead of wood, gold, and hubris. A floating fortress bristling with cannons, smeared with the royal grandeur designed not only for combating the enemies, but also to assert Sweden's growing dominance over the Baltic. Thousands gathered along the waterfront, their eyes fixed on the ship. Anticipation hung heavy in the air. The Vasa was more than just a warship: it was a very idea made flesh, or rather, an idea almost collapsing from the weight of its own ambition. Ironically, a gust of wind picked up its sails. The ship tilted to one side, swayed about for an instant and heeled once again. Water poured in through the open gunports. In a few minutes, the *Vasa*—the pride of Sweden's navy—sank less than a mile from shore, vanishing under the waves in full view of the stunned crowd. The disaster was swift, embarrassing, and perhaps the most damning: entirely avoidable.

Why had Sweden's most advanced warship failed so catastrophically? It wasn't just a ship designed to sail; it was meant to be a spectacle, a towering symbol of imperial might. Worse still, the king insisted on two gun decks with heavy armament—a requirement that dramatically affected the center of gravity. The shipbuilders likely understood the ship's instability; after all, it nearly capsized during a stability test, but no one dared defy the king's ambitious timeline. After all, who contradicts a king? Sweden's rulers, intoxicated by their swelling influence, sought to fashion a ship so formidable in appearance that it might—perhaps—defy the physics that govern all things.

The answer, as it turned out, was glaringly simple: it was an engineering failure of monumental proportions. Beneath the grandiosity, beneath the gilded carvings and statues, lurked a fatal miscalculation—the ship was top-heavy. Designed to impress, it couldn't withstand its own weight. It had been built to be seen, not sailed. The sea—and the laws of physics—had other plans. About 30 people died in the disaster.

The *Vasa* remained entombed in brackish Baltic silt for more than three centuries—a silent monument to excess and error. When raised in 1961, it emerged nearly intact, its ornately carved timbers defying time itself. Today it looms over visitors at Stockholm's Vasa Museum, a relic not only of a vanished empire but of a universal truth: ignore reality at your peril. The ship was majestic, yes—but physics is unimpressed by majesty.

— **Further Reading** —

Sandström, Birgitta, *Vasa: The Story of a Swedish Warship*. Collins, 1988.

Chapter 27 The Tally Fire of London

Nothing Left but the Smell of Smoke

In the year 1834, the British government came to own two cartloads of old "tally sticks," ancient wooden paddles used for recording financial transactions. These tools are inscribed with notches to signify debts and credits, now relics of a bygone era.

They were once useful, but like many such old gadgets, they had rightfully fallen into complete disuse. Surely, the question remained, what is the next step in dealing with remnants from an earlier, slower era? As we would soon learn, the decision was both misguided and disastrous. Instead of just destroying or burying these in some corner of forgotten artifacts, somebody, —no doubt with the very best of intentions, suggested that they be burnt in the House of Lords furnace.

It seems almost absurd in retrospect, the thought that the government, perhaps eager to rid itself of these artifacts, would choose such an inappropriate means of disposal.

The results were disastrous. The small, humble furnace wasn't designed to have such a large volume of fuel thrown into it, and it soon was overwhelmed. The flames spread, and what was going to be a small event soon became a catastrophe.

The wooden structure around the furnace ignited from the heat of the blaze. It was noticed by staff too late, and most of the Palace of Westminster was consumed in fire. The House of Lords, the House of Commons, and much of the medieval complex, buildings steeped in centuries of history, were lost to the flames. Tragedy and irony: the very seat of British governance in a sense collapsed under its own outdated bureaucracy, a victim of past and present colliding at catastrophic force.

It was not just a fire: it was a failure of imagination, a lapse in foresight. Even when the scientific method had begun remolding human understanding of the world, failure to project the impact of that apparently innocuous decision would have proved just how insulated the most rational systems can be from the evidence of poor attention to detail. Once ignited, fire did not consume a building; it devoured the very foundations of British political life and imposed a monumental effort towards reengineering. As William Shatner said in the film *Airplane II,* "Irony can be pretty ironic sometimes."

The Gothic Revival design chosen to replace the destroyed buildings became perennial in changing the architectural expression of power in the UK. This was always the dream of an ambitious rebuilding process led by Sir Charles Barry and Augustus Pugin, but at the heavy historical cost of what was lost in the fire.

In the days that followed, crowds milled along the banks of the River Thames, taking in the spectacle of the utter destruction of their houses of government.

Now it is very easy to perceive such a fire as just another freak of fate—accidental disaster by bureaucratic incompetence. But behind all this lies a fact that is even weightier than historical curiosity: that fire reminds us how easily systems, however rationally governed, become blind to their own negligence. Progress is often imagined as a straight line, when in reality it's a jagged path where past and present collide explosively.

Though outshone by many more famous disasters in British history such as the Great Fire of London, this event deserves our study, specifically as a lesson in forward thinking, the limits of human judgment, and the vulnerability of our institutions. Much was destroyed by fire, but something new was also born. In that sense, it does not differ from scientific understanding of how science advances internally: collapse of old systems by burning, destroying what no longer serves, to create openness to something better. But, as we're always reminded, progress has its price.[17]

— Further Reading —

Jones, Christopher, *Great Palace: Story of Parliament.* BBC Books, 1983.

Chapter 28 The Great Stink

The Smell That Stopped London

In the sweltering summer of 1858, London found itself ensnared in a sensory nightmare of its own making. Once again along the River Thames, once the city's shimmering artery of life, had degenerated into a slow-moving, viscous mass of human refuse. A brutal heatwave ensured that no one, from the slums of Southwark to the halls of Westminster, could escape the assault. The air was thick with the putrid exhalations of centuries of civic negligence, a stench so vile that Parliamentarians, in a rare moment of bipartisanship, doused their curtains in chloride of lime in a desperate act of olfactory triage. Some, succumbing to the logic of survival, proposed abandoning Westminster entirely until nature—or providence—provided relief.

But this was no act of god, no inscrutable decree from the heavens. The Great Stink was the inevitable consequence of an ancient city outpacing its own infrastructure, of a population explosion shackled to an excremental system more befitting a medieval hamlet than a burgeoning metropolis. The logic was brutally simple: waste was disposed of by the easiest means available, which, in London's case, meant direct deposit into the Thames. For decades, this arrangement had been an open secret: a tacit agreement between the city and its own filth. But reality, as it often does, eventually presented the bill. Cholera and typhoid fever, unseen yet ruthless, harvested their victims with mechanical indifference, while the very river that had once quenched London's thirst became its most efficient vector of death.

Science, however, has a habit of cutting through the fog of superstition and inertia. The Great Stink, though a catastrophe of the nose, became an inflection point for reason. Parliament, forced into action by the sheer inescapability of the crisis, finally sanctioned the construction of a modern sewage system. The task fell to Joseph Bazalgette, a man whose genius lay not in lofty rhetoric but in brick, mortar, and an unwavering grasp of first principles. His subterranean network of tunnels, hidden beneath the feet of millions, became the unheralded circulatory system of a cleaner, healthier London: an engineering triumph whose benefits persist to this day.

Thus, a grotesque reality collided with human ingenuity, and in the end, reason prevailed. The Great Stink was a visceral reminder that civilization does not merely advance by accident or divine favor but by the relentless application of knowledge to necessity. And if there is a lesson to be drawn from the fetid streets of 19th-century London, it is that truth, whether scientific, moral, or sanitary, demands recognition, no matter how unpleasant it may first appear.

— Further Reading —

Wohl, Anthony S., *Endangered Lives: Public Health in Victorian Britain. Harvard University Press*, 1983.

Chapter 29 The Great Balloon Disaster

A Cold Flight to Nowhere

The Swedish adventurer S. A. Andrée, in 1897, apparently was successful in embarking on the most glorious hubris-laden mission that became a timeless reminder of the fragility of human endeavor. He was to be the first to reach the North Pole by air, something that nowadays seems more mythical than achievable. Andrée launched the *Örnen*, an "aerostat" full of hydrogen from Spitsbergen in the Arctic Circle, with two partners. The hope was sublime and simple: that the forces of nature, the very winds themselves, would carry them across the polar wastes and to the North Pole, the prize that had eluded explorers for centuries.

In its fickle and cruel way, the wind did not cooperate. The *Örnen*'s journey began as it ought: hopeful, optimistic, proving the ingenuity of man. Yet, as the balloon drifted over the ice, the unpredictable weather patterns of the Arctic started to show the folly of human confidence. Within a few short hours, the winds turned and wrenched the aeronauts off course; soon, they were at the mercy of a wrathful and indifferent environment.

The weather turned stormy, and the capacity of men and their flimsy vessel was affected. Within days, the balloon was reduced to just another casualty of the Arctic's brutality, forced to ground on ice floes, their planned ascent to the pole obliterated. The geography of the Arctic is unforgiving, yes, but what of the human error that often precedes it? Here, even the most brilliant minds and bodies finally fall: extreme temperatures, incessant snowstorms, and icy vastness. Did they not leave themselves with limited supplies, so that when inevitable failure began, they were already doomed? Now, the men had no choice but to traverse the frozen wasteland on foot, dragging their bulky equipment, hoping against reason that they could find their way back to civilization. But the ice had no mercy. What could the men do when their bodies were failing, when the world they once thought they could conquer was suddenly unrelenting in its indifference to their struggle? They were too far gone, their weaknesses too obvious in the face of the raw force of nature. With the finality that only such a place can deliver, the men died. Their bodies, like too many before them on polar quests, were lost to the silent, vast nothingness.

For decades, their fates remained a historical enigma, wrapped in the frozen mystery of that tragic balloon. The *Örnen* itself, once seen as the instrument of human ingenuity, vanished, and the world was left to speculate. The question that hung over the tragedy wasn't just about what happened, but about why. Why does ambition, even at its most extreme, falter so easily when confronted by the sheer scale of nature's indifference? The answers, elusive as they were, did not arrive until 1930, when a team of explorers uncovered the remnants of the lost expedition. It was their last camp, found on the island of Kvitøya in Svalbard.

What they uncovered was more than just the bodies of the men: they found the diaries, those fragile remnants of human thought, offering insight into the last days of the men's struggle. They spoke of pain and confusion, of perseverance against increasing desperation. In the end, Andrée's balloon was perhaps remembered more for its failure than its boldness or success. It had become, rather than a testimony to what the human spirit could achieve, a testimony to some harsh truths that most of us often ignore: nature has little interest in human ambitions, that we are terribly small, and that the best we can do with our reason can be scattered by something we cannot control.

— Further Reading —

Capelotti, P. J., *By Airship to the North Pole: An Archaeology of Human Exploration*. Rutgers University Press, 1999.

Chapter 30 South Fork Dam Catastrophe

Drowning in Indifference

The Johnstown Flood of 1889 was not merely a disaster of nature, but a catastrophe of human arrogance: an engineered apocalypse authored by the apathy of the wealthy. The South Fork Dam, once a robust structure, had been purchased and tampered with by the South Fork Fishing and Hunting Club, an enclave of Pittsburgh's industrial elite. Among its members were Andrew Carnegie, Henry Clay Frick, and Andrew Mellon, men whose fortunes were built upon mastery of steel, finance, and calculated neglect. The terms *cold-heartedness* and *inhumanity* also come to mind.

For them, the dam was no longer an engineering necessity to protect the town below, but a mere inconvenience: an obstacle to be reshaped for their leisure. They lowered its height to accommodate a wider road, ensuring smoother passage for their carriages but weakening the structure's very integrity. They removed crucial drainage systems, *sluice pipes*, dismissing them as superfluous, and failed to install proper spillway screens, allowing debris to accumulate unchecked. These were not oversights; they were choices, made with the serene confidence that consequences were for *other* men to bear. Not "We, the elite."

Warnings came, again and again; engineers and townspeople sounded the alarm, pleading that the dam was a looming specter of destruction. The club, however, did nothing.

Then came the rains. For days, water swelled behind the compromised barrier until, at last, on May 31, 1889, the dam surrendered. What followed was not a flood in the simple sense, but a liquid avalanche, a thunderous collapse of civilization itself. A wave roared down the valley, obliterating Johnstown and erasing over 2,200 lives in its path.

And yet, in the aftermath of this corporate manslaughter, there were no guilty men. The laws of Pennsylvania, sculpted to shield the powerful, held that negligence, no matter how egregious, was not a crime. Survivors sought justice, but the courts, in their infinite servility, sided with the architects of ruin. No reparations were paid. No sentences were served. The men who had reshaped a dam for their own ease had, in effect, written an obituary for an entire town; and they did so without consequence. Carnegie, though not directly involved in the dam's management, later donated money to rebuild Johnstown, possibly as a way to ease public anger and guilt over the disaster. So who were these men, really?

Carnegie: full of hypocrisy and moral contradictions. (We'll cover Carnegie in Part 3 of this book.)

Mellon: insidiously selfish. As U.S. Treasury Secretary (1921-1932), he shaped tax policies that benefited the ultra-rich and contributed to the wealth inequality leading to the Great Depression.

Henry Clay Frick: seething with raw, violent ruthlessness. In another incident, he ordered Pinkertons to break the steelworkers' strike of 1892, leading to a bloody battle with several deaths. He was the kind of man who quite frankly didn't give a *frick* about other people's lives. To sum him up in Dr. Seuss words: "a foul one; a nasty, wasty skunk."

The Johnstown Flood remains one of the deadliest man-made disasters in U.S. history.

— Further Reading —
McCullough, David, *The Johnstown Flood*. Simon & Schuster, 1987.

— Easy Viewing —
History Channel, "I Was There: The Deadliest Flood in American History." www.youtube.com/watch?v=Zj2v5Akm1Bg

Chapter 31 The Halifax Explosion

A Tragedy of Unimaginable Proportions.

On December 6th, 1917, the city of Halifax, in Nova Scotia, was struck by one of history's greatest human-induced catastrophes. It was as if the very sound of the blast penetrated the fog so thick hanging over ordinary Halifax life, razing the place to the ground. What had happened was a simple tragic mistake. The French munitions ship *Mont-Blanc* was in collision with the Norwegian vessel *Imo* in the harbor. In a second, the *Mont-Blanc* caught fire, setting off a fast ignition of her highly volatile cargo into an explosive chain reaction of horrendous consequences.

The force of the explosion absolutely *leveled* much of Halifax, killing almost 2,000 people at once, while thousands more bore harrowing injuries from the blast. It not only reached the city's outskirts but the blast traveled up to 160 kilometers, shattering windows and rattling homes to leave the wider region stunned with the havoc wrought by disaster. There was more damage than that: the explosion triggered a tsunami rushing through the harbor, crashing chaos down upon already impossible destruction.

After such a tragedy, the comforting thought arises that it was an accident: the *Mont-Blanc* was just in the wrong place at the wrong time, and merely some accident caused all this mayhem. The deeper, more uncomfortable truth is that this explosion resulted from a systemic failure. The *Mont-Blanc* was carrying dangerous explosive cargo, and the movements of the ship through the harbor were, quite literally, an accident waiting to happen. Industrial practices, predicated on lowering costs and maximizing efficiency, made Halifax a ticking time bomb; the tragedy is not only the explosion, but the systemic neglect that allowed this to happen.

Aid poured in from the neighboring communities and as far away as Boston, yet the city's medical infrastructure was stretched well beyond capacity and struggled to provide even the most basic cure.

From an unanticipated disaster like this emerged the sheer complexity of human suffering: burns, shattered bones, crushed organs, being a reality check on the limits of science and humanitarian response.

What exists, in the end, is a testament to our scientific and existential reminder that our systems of modern life are fragile, even brittle, often just a single spark away from catastrophe. The Halifax Explosion may have been an error, a blind spot in the machinery of war, but it speaks to something deeper: it is not a single fault that creates the potential for disaster, but rather the confluence of errors, negligence, and the inherent risk of doing too much, too fast, without truly realizing the consequences.

— Further Reading —

Kitz, Janet F., *Shattered City: The Halifax Explosion and the Road to Recovery*. Nimbus Publishing, 1989.

Pyke, Josh., *Explosion in Halifax Harbour: The Illustrated History of a Disaster That Shook the World*. Formac Publishing, 1994.

Chapter 32 The St. Francis Dam Collapse

March 12, 1928, was the kind of night that witnessed the termination of bureaucratic negligence by the overt effectiveness of physics, the latter favoring its cause as it oftentimes does. The St. Francis Dam, a towering slab of miscalculated confidence, gave way just before midnight, unleashing unimaginable torrents that carved a path through the San Francisquito Canyon. The flood was more like an extermination: water, propelled onward in an unblinking fashion by pure gravity, swept aside towns and trees, livestock, and human beings with an equal sense of indifference. Officially, over 450 perished, though, given the scale of the devastation, one suspects that the accountants of the dead may have lost count.

The flood, churning with debris and the occasional unfortunate house, roared toward the Pacific, leaving in its wake a moonscape where towns once stood. Fillmore, in particular, fared poorly, its residents forced to confront the sort of existential questions that arise when one's home is unexpectedly relocated several miles downstream. The survivors, stunned and drenched, emerged into a world that bore no resemblance to the one in which they had gone to bed.

The cause? A cavalcade of avoidable errors. The dam, as it turned out, had been built atop unstable ground, a fact known to some but ignored by many, because optimism is cheaper than caution. Cracks had begun to appear in the days leading up to the collapse: cracks which, in the grand tradition of institutional insolence, were deemed unworthy of concern.

In the aftermath, a certain amount of hand-wringing ensued. Laws were passed, committees convened, and suddenly, engineers were expected to take geology somewhat seriously. It was, in many ways, the St. Francis Dam's final contribution to society: a cautionary tale about what happens when blind ambition meets indifferent reality. The lesson was simple: when building a dam, it helps to ensure that the ground beneath it isn't inclined to move about.

— Further Reading —

Wilkman, Jon, *Floodpath: The Deadliest Man-Made Disaster of 20th-Century America and the Making of Modern Los Angeles*. Bloomsbury Press, 2016.

Chapter 33 The Great Emu War

Australia was not only enduring drought and an economic depression in 1932; it was undergoing an epic existential battle: the struggle to survive against emus. That's right, emus. Those giant, flightless birds that are mostly associated with running really fast and looking goofily cute. The emus migrated into Western Australia's wheat belt in huge numbers and made life miserable for farmers, having traveled hundreds of miles in search of food. After an exceptionally bad drought, the emus started to think, "Hey, let's enter into these wheat fields and make a buffet out of them." And that's exactly what they did. There was no concern about your crops, livelihood of farmers, carefully laid agricultural plans. All they cared about was that they were in there to eat, and they meant business.

Of course, any reasonable government, when faced with such a crisis, would do what they could do: call in the military. We're talking machine guns. Yes, you read that right: machine guns. Armed to the teeth and oozing with confidence that they could bring down these oversized Aussi chickens, the Australian army marched into the fields, ready to do battle under the command of Major G.P.W. Meredith. This, of course, led to the first and probably most important lesson of the Great Emu War: emus are fast.

Shooting at emus, it turns out, is just like trying to hit a moving target on a treadmill; except set the treadmill on fire and make the target constantly dodge left and right as you fumble with malfunctioning weapons. The speed and uncanny ability of the emus to scatter at the least provocation made the soldiers seem to be playing a game of "Where's Waldo?" in a field of wheat.

The operation was eventually abandoned in embarrassment after poor results and political backlash. That's right, folks: the emus won. The birds managed to defend themselves from one of the most ridiculous military engagements ever to take place, forcing the Australian government to terminate the military offensive and go back into more peaceful and less ridiculous methods to cope with the problem, like fencing subsidies and bounties on emus.

It was, in the end, curiously humbling. The Great Emu War would prove, then, two things: 1. Emus are tougher than they look, and 2. Sometimes, Nature really gets the last laugh.

— Further Reading —

Evans, C.J., *The Great Emu War: Or How Australia Lost A War Against Birds*. (Independently published) 2018.

Chapter 34 USS Akron

Another Tragic Airship Disaster

On April 4, 1933, this airship fell very quickly and violently, not because it was so big, but because it was so unreasonably fragile for its size and dimensions. The USS *Akron* was helium-filled, so it wasn't going to blow up like the Hindenburg. The huge airship held its own airplanes, like a flying aircraft carrier, and found itself at the mercy of a storm it could not withstand. This did not take place in the wilds of America. No, this was the middle of a routine training exercise, hundreds of feet above the New Jersey coastline, until nature itself turned on it, and the airship came apart at the seams.

You might think that an airship capable of carrying five planes in its hull would have been the cutting edge of military technology. And in 1933, it was. Its triangular trusses were fashioned from a new lightweight alloy, duralumin 17-SRT. But you also might think that a machine that large, designed to ride the sky, would have taken a few more factors into account: like, say, the fact that skies don't always play nice. What happened when the *Akron* got caught in an unrelenting storm? Well, imagine trying to fly a paper kite in a hurricane, and you get the gist.

Despite the best efforts of the crew, who were almost certainly hoping that their grand engineering experiment would survive, the *Akron* lost its battle with wind and weather. It snapped apart in mid-air, like a toy torn apart by an angry child. Of the 76 people aboard, only three made it out alive. Rear Admiral William Moffett, a man who had spent years selling the idea of airships to anyone who would listen, was among the dead. So was the very technology he had believed in.

The odd thing? No one really seems to remember this. The *Akron* disaster doesn't have the dramatic flair of the Hindenburg's fiery end, which seems to have burned its image into the collective memory, complete with newsreel footage and iconic imagery. The Akron was just another casualty of the rapid pace of technology, a transition from dirigibles to airplanes, a moment when it became clear that airships were on the way out, and airplanes were about to take over the skies.

The *Akron* saga could have been passed off as yet another obscure historical footnote: a tragic failure of a grand idea. But the memory lingers; a remembrance of the fickleness of invention. The Navy canceled the airship program on the grounds that airplanes were simply more storm-resilient. The *Akron*, too grand for its time and too delicate for the winds that ravaged it, is the sort of forgotten disaster that happens when progress comes a little too fast for its own good.[18]

USS Akron

Chapter 35 The New London School Explosion

On March 18, 1937, a town in East Texas, so quiet and unassuming, was thrust into the pages of history by an event as tragic as it was absurd. New London, Texas, population unknown and perhaps irrelevant, became the scene of one of the deadliest school disasters in the history of the United States, even worse than your typical weekly school shootings today.

It was here, on an otherwise ordinary afternoon, that the New London School, a building that looked no different from any other on a dusty street, was swallowed by an explosion so violent it felt like the end of the world had come knocking. The loss? At least 295 lives, most of them children, and hundreds more bearing injuries that would shape their lives forever.

So how does a seemingly mundane educational institution turn into the site of such catastrophe? A simple thing, really: a gas leak. No ordinary gas leak: it seemed to harbor a sinister air of almost often deliberate malice. Natural gas had been building up silently and unnoticed, deprived of color and odor, during days or perhaps weeks, forming like some malevolent ghost in the air. Somewhere in the sparks, probably within the electrical system, this invisible evil ignited and the whole school: its walls, desks, and hope were obliterated in a flash of a terrifying power.

Imagine it. It was a complete wreck, from a building into a heap of bricks and timber, and the very air thick with confusion and despair. You might have imagined that the survivors, their shock and disbelief just developing, were really carried away in some nonsensical dream from which they would awaken shortly. But no. The rubble was real. The death toll, staggering. The survivors, in a cruel twist of fate, were not only forced to deal with the physical destruction but with a profound emotional wreckage, one that would forever alter their small community's fabric.

The rescue efforts that followed were, at best, frustratingly insufficient. With the entire school full of life and promise suddenly reduced to dust, what can one possibly do? Transitional days came and went. People, many of them strangers from nearby towns, crawled through the debris; some in futile hopes of finding someone alive, while others only wished to bear witness to the incomprehensible loss. But the truth of the matter is that this was not just an unfortunate twist of fate. It was just a failure to observe basic precautions, a complete disregard for safety measures so simple we ought to have known better than to ignore them. A faulty gas line and an unheeded warning, and the result was sheer devastation.

What followed was a slow reckoning: a quiet but deliberate shift toward better safety regulations, though not without the all-too-typical delay that always accompanies meaningful reform. It wasn't until this disaster forced the nation's hand that there was any real effort to implement comprehensive gas leak detection systems and more rigorous standards for the maintenance of such systems in public buildings. The New London explosion, now just a distant echo in the minds of many, serves as a grim reminder of how fragile safety can be and how even in the most mundane moments, the smallest oversight can lead to the greatest of catastrophes.

— Further Reading —
Green, Bobby, *Gone at 3:17: The Untold Story of the Worst School Disaster in American History*. University of Texas Press, 2012.

Chapter 36 Hindenburg

I'll bet you've heard of this one. The year 1937, of course, will stand forever with a strange kind of tragedy, the very sort which, in its own infinity of ingenuity, is so prone to, let's say, "humanity." On May 6, the LZ 129 *Hindenburg* blew up. One might think the cosmos were commenting on our very human desire to conquer the skies. The disaster occurred just off the shore of Lakehurst, New Jersey, as the bright behemoth descended toward a landing, silhouetted against the dying light of the day. A giant in every measure, it became the scene for a tragic spectacle, one in which 36 victims succumbed to flames hot enough that it would seem the gods themselves were amused by the folly of mortals.

There is, of course, the ever-present question: why? Why, in an age of extraordinary technological strides, was this marvel of man's hubristic tendencies still inflated with hydrogen, that volatile and unstable gas, rather than helium, the *non-combustible* alternative? The answer, naturally, is wrapped in a fog of geopolitical necessity. Helium was in the hands of the United States, which, fearing its use in military applications, had placed it under strict export controls. The United States has historically been the Saudi Arabia of helium, with the gas being trapped along with methane ("natural gas") in mines mostly in the Texas, Oklahoma, and Kansas.

And so, the Germans, with typical practicality, chose hydrogen. It was cheap, abundant, and so devastatingly flammable that its very presence in an airship should have been enough to deter anyone with even the faintest understanding of chemistry.

Strange as it seems, the crash itself, though horrific, was not entirely without its redeeming features. The *Hindenburg*, by some twist of fate, was relatively close to the ground when disaster struck. It was, if we can use the term, a "fortunate" kind of failure. Passengers, sensing the flames, rushed to windows, scrambled through open hatches, and in some rare cases, found themselves tumbling to safety. One can almost hear the commentary of hindsight: "Not a perfect escape plan, but certainly better than most." The rapidity with which the fire spread allowed the unfortunate souls aboard no time to suffer a prolonged agony, even as it reduced the massive structure to an ash heap.

But it is the legacy of the *Hindenburg* that remains forever etched in the collective consciousness. Hardly anyone remembers the *Graf Zeppelin* (which was mentioned by Marilyn Monroe in *Some Like It Hot*), or the USS *Akron*; no one recalls the grand, languid voyages of these dirigibles across the sky. What endures, inexorably, is the image of a flaming airship crashing to the ground in a death knell for the great age of airships. The *Hindenburg*, a monument to engineering pomposity and strategic oversight, becomes a lesson in how, despite our best intentions, the seemingly most invulnerable of structures can be reduced to dust by the simplest of miscalculations.

And who can forget the words of that distraught reporter, "Oh, the humanity!" echoed again in 1992 by Garth in the movie *Wayne's World?*

— Further Reading —

Tarshis, Lauren, *I Survived the Hindenburg Disaster, 1937.* Scholastic, 2016.

McCarthy, Michael, *The Hidden Hindenburg: The Untold Story of the Tragedy, the Nazi Secrets, and the Quest to Rule the Skies.* Lyons Press, 2020.

Chapter 37 The Tacoma Narrows Bridge Collapse

A Bridge, a Breeze, a Disaster

On November 7, 1940, the world was treated to a performance, the kind which would become forcedly, if not unhappy, iconic in a delineation of what happens when the whimsical tone of engineering hits the unfriendly whim of weather. There, over Tacoma, Washington, the notorious Tacoma Narrows Bridge, i.e. "Galloping Gertie," broke apart in a dramatic, nearly theatrical event of collapse, leaving the public quite horrified but somehow fascinated by it. It had only been four months after the completion of the bridge. The engineers' optimism was misplaced, as was the fragile disposition of the design of the bridge.

However, the Tacoma Narrows Bridge was not built by a group of reckless novices. It was, in serious engineering minds, a serious project. But here was the twist: much like many man-made things, it was born out of hubris; this particular case was an egregious oversight of the simplest of forces: wind. The engineers might have been thinking too highly of their own brilliance that they failed to consider how much damage innocent-feeling winds could do to a structure like this one. With the lack of proper dampening mechanisms to resist the forces at play, the bridge became a helpless participator in its own destruction.

The winds sustained at a brisk 40 miles per hour, and had their way with the bridge, creating a series of oscillations that went from mildly disconcerting to, ultimately, disastrous. The bridge began to twist, sway, and undulate in a manner that would become known as spectacularly grotesque, unable to cope with the increasingly resonant forces. The last act was quick. The center part of the bridge, undone by its own neglect to take winds into account, finally folded inside itself in a burst of twisted metal and fractured concrete.

As unlikely as it sounds, there were no fatalities. An unholy miracle, maybe. The footage of the collapse recorded with that kind of nakedness which black-and-white film can capture lives on into perpetuity, even echoing as a terrible reminder to engineers and the public alike that the most powerful structures carry their weakest fatality. The disaster left a painful imprint on the economy and pride of Tacoma, but perhaps the more grievous loss was to the reputation of the engineers, which has become and forever will be linked with the display of their own failure.

However, progress came from this. The collapse of "Galloping Gertie" was the awakening call engineers needed to heed. It prompted a rethink in the design of suspension bridges, resulting in more extensive tests for wind resistance and well-founded calculations of the forces in play. What started as an embarrassing dumb mistake eventually evolved into a lesson that would redesign the future of bridge engineering. In the long term, it was a reminder to man that despite his innovations, there will always be a factor of nature, quietly lurking in the background, ready to expose his vulnerabilities. Sometimes, as shown by "Galloping Gertie," it may even prove catastrophic, leaving behind disasters.

— Further Reading —

Abler, Amanda, *Galloping Gertie: The True Story of the Tacoma Narrows Bridge Collapse*. Little Bigfoot, 2021.

— Easy Viewing —

Short video: www.youtube.com/watch?v=XggxeuFDaDU

Chapter 38 The Kyshtym Disaster

Fallout, Cover-ups, and Cold War Chaos

Long before Chernobyl turned the phrase "nuclear disaster" into a household term, the Soviets had already managed to irradiate vast swaths of their own countryside in a spectacularly ill-conceived game of atomic hot potato. The Kyshtym Disaster of 1957 was, to put it politely, an unqualified catastrophe. To put it less politely, it was the sort of blunder that could only happen when a government with a deep-seated allergy to admitting mistakes meets an industrial complex that considers safety precautions an optional afterthought.

The story goes like this: at the Mayak Nuclear Fuel Reprocessing Plant—an operation so secret that it might as well have been on the far side of the moon—a tank filled with radioactive waste decided it had had enough. It exploded. Not with a dramatic mushroom cloud or any of the Hollywood flourishes one might expect from a nuclear calamity, but with a more bureaucratically nightmarish sort of destruction: one that spread radioactive isotopes across 10,000 square kilometers, effectively turning the region into an open-air science experiment in human endurance.

The Soviet response was, in a word, Soviet. Evacuations? Yes, but without explanations. The people told to leave their homes had no idea they were fleeing from an invisible, deadly menace. Those left behind weren't so much as given a pamphlet on radiation poisoning. And naturally, officials decided the best way to deal with the disaster was to pretend it didn't exist. When it eventually became impossible to ignore, they named it after Kyshtym, a town that had nothing to do with the disaster, because acknowledging Mayak would have been too honest for comfort.

For decades, no one outside the Soviet Union even knew it had happened. Only in the 1980s, when the USSR itself was beginning to wobble under the weight of its own deceptions, did the truth start to leak out. By then, the damage was done. Thousands of lives had been shortened, entire villages abandoned, and the local wildlife had almost certainly developed some deeply unwholesome mutations.

The Kyshtym Disaster, in the end, was less a singular tragedy and more a case study in how not to run a nuclear program, or, indeed, a country. It's a sobering reminder that sometimes the most dangerous force in the world isn't radiation. It's bureaucracy.

— Further Reading —
Medvedev, Zhores, *Nuclear Disaster in the Urals.* W. W. Norton & Company, 1980.

Chapter 39 Beach Bang Bingo: Let's Blow Up A Whale

There are bad ideas, and then there's "let's blow up a whale." You've probably seen this fiasco on the internet, a masterstroke of the Oregon Highway Division in 1970. This was an era when civic problem-solving apparently involved looking at a rotting, 8-ton sea creature and deciding the best course of action was to make it airborne. Why bury it? Why drag it to sea? When you have half a ton of dynamite lying around, the only reasonable thing to do, if you're the sort of person who played with fireworks a little too enthusiastically as a child, is to strap it to the whale and hope for the best.

The plan, if you can call it that, hinged on the idea that a precisely measured explosion would delicately convert the whale into a fine mist of seagull food. What actually happened was that an enormous, supremely dead marine mammal was transformed into a high-velocity meat storm. When the explosives were detonated, instead of neatly disassembling the whale, the blast turned it into a skyborne catastrophe. Chunks of blubber the size of beanbag chairs were launched into the stratosphere before plummeting back to Earth with an alarming commitment to gravity. One particularly ambitious hunk traveled a full quarter-mile before the laws of physics brought it to rest atop an unfortunate man's car, which, it should be noted, was parked well outside what authorities had assured him was the "danger zone."

Incredibly, nobody was killed, though many were left reconsidering their trust in government competence. The cleanup, which was supposed to be avoided entirely, became infinitely worse, as giant hunks of greasy whale meat now had to be collected from buildings, roads, and possibly a few deeply traumatized locals. To this day, the Exploding Whale Incident remains one of the finest examples of human ingenuity being completely and magnificently misapplied. It also serves as a valuable life lesson: when faced with a logistical problem, consider all options before landing on "detonate."

— **Easy Viewing** —

See a short video created by the KATU 2 News crew here: www.youtube.com/watch?v=V6CLumsir34

Chapter 40 The Banqiao Dam Failure

A Catastrophic Collapse in China

In the year 1975, the Banqiao Dam in Henan Province, China, fell victim to a horrible and inevitable calamity in the course of this perfect storm of bureaucratic ineptitude, engineering miscalculation, and atmospheric indifference. That is, it was more a monument to ideological vanity than a triumph of hydrological engineering: it was part of Maoist China's ambitious but wildly misguided campaign to bring nature to heel before political power. It was, to borrow an apt phrase, a catastrophe foretold.

The dam's architects, laboring under the delusion that ideology could substitute for expertise, had built a structure incapable of withstanding the forces it was meant to tame. When a typhoon arrived, delivering nearly a year's worth of rainfall in a matter of days, the dam's purported defenses proved as substantive as a bureaucrat's promise. The reservoir swelled beyond its limits, and at the moment of critical failure, the structure collapsed under the weight of its own contradictions.

What ensued was destruction on an imperial scale. A wall of water obliterated entire villages, sweeping away homes, factories, and whatever passed for modern infrastructure. In a grimly efficient demonstration of cascading failure, at least 62 additional dams downstream suffered similar fates, amplifying the catastrophe. Official estimates cite a death toll of 170,000, though such numbers, tidily rounded and state-approved, are less likely to represent reality than to serve as damage control. Those not killed immediately faced an aftermath marked by famine, disease, and a level of human suffering beyond the capacity of government-issued euphemisms to conceal.

Yet, for years, concealment was precisely the strategy. The Chinese government, ever attuned to the optics of disaster, classified the Banqiao calamity as a "natural accident," an Orwellian turn of phrase that absolved planners and policymakers of culpability. Only decades later did the truth emerge: the Banqiao Dam disaster was not an act of God, but an act of man: specifically, of men who believed that physics, hydrology, and meteorology were mere subordinates to ideology.

The catastrophe stands as an enduring indictment of authoritarian governance: a system in which expertise is subordinated to obedience, inconvenient facts are massaged into oblivion, and the lessons of history are more likely to be buried than heeded. If history is any guide, the greatest threat to human civilization is not nature's indifference, but our own willful ignorance of it.

— Further Reading —

Horner, Lana, *Banqiao Dam Failure: The Collapse That Cost Thousands of Lives.* (Independently published) 2024.

Lee, Seungho, *China's Water Resources Management: A Long March to Sustainability*. Palgrave Macmillan, 2014.

Chapter 41 Draining Lake Peigneur

A Drilling Disaster

One might have hoped that in a country so enamored with its own industrial prowess, the basic principles of geology would have received a passing nod. Alas, in 1980, a group of oil drillers in Louisiana set about proving otherwise in what would become the Lake Peigneur Disaster, an event so staggeringly miscalculated that it would have been hilarious if not for its apocalyptic consequences.

The masterminds in question, working for Texaco, managed to do something truly remarkable: they turned a perfectly ordinary lake into a raging sinkhole by mistakenly perforating the ceiling of an underground salt mine. Now, one might assume that, given the choice, no one would willingly place a fragile excavation site beneath an active drilling operation, but that would be to underestimate the astonishing optimism of American industry.[19]

The ensuing disaster was biblical in scale and Kafkaesque in its bureaucratic oversight. The lake, clearly unprepared for such an indignity, reacted by doing its best impression of a bathtub emptying. Water cascaded downward with such force that it dragged eleven barges, acres of land, and anything else foolish enough to be nearby into the subterranean void. The mine itself, presumably baffled by the sudden and unexpected deluge, promptly collapsed. Meanwhile, engineers and executives scrambled about, undoubtedly forming committees and issuing memos long after their equipment had already been swallowed whole.

And then, in an astonishing display of cosmic irony, the water surged back in with enough force to create the tallest waterfall in Louisiana's history, a geological middle finger directed squarely at human incompetence. The lake, now permanently altered, took on an entirely new ecosystem—one that, incidentally, had no particular use for Texaco.

No one perished, though one suspects that several careers did. Today, the Lake Peigneur Disaster stands as a testament to the perils of industrial arrogance and the unshakable fact that the Earth, when provoked, has a dark sense of humor.

— Further Reading —

Gautreaux Jacob, *64 Parishes.* "Lake Peigneur Drilling Accident." July 28, 2023.
> 64parishes.org/entry/lake-peigneur-drilling-accident

Chapter 42 The Gladys Positioning System

Once upon a time—not in a fairy tale, but in that vaguely authoritarian phase of mid-20th-century America where everything was beige and people still smoked at their desks—humans decided they were tired of being lost. It simply wouldn't do. Being lost was inefficient, undignified, and, worse, made meetings late. So naturally, they built a constellation of mechanical sky-nannies to keep track of themselves.

This, dear reader, became GPS: a system so mind-warpingly complex that its mere continued operation suggests either the divine hand of order or the sheer brute force of bureaucratic inertia.

The system works like this: tiny clocks orbit the Earth at marginally relativistic speeds, so they experience time slightly differently than we do, which is either poetic or mildly disturbing, depending on how much coffee you've had. These clocks beam out their existential angst to your phone, which uses the subtle differences in arrival times to decide that yes, you *are* standing just outside a Taco Bell, probably regretting your life choices.

But the real star of the show is *not* the satellites, not the generals, not the parade of pale men in crew cuts. It's Dr. Gladys West.

Gladys West is the sort of person who quietly saves civilization while wearing sensible shoes. In 1956, she was hired by the U.S. Navy, not to fire cannons or plot invasions, but to do something far more daunting: figure out the exact shape of a planet that's spent 4.5 billion years stubbornly refusing to be a perfect sphere.

The Earth, as it turns out, is shaped like someone sat on it: uneven, bulgy, squashed, slouching slightly to the left. And if you want to know where you are *on* it using satellites *above* it, you better get those bumps and wobbles right.

Gladys got them right.

She waded into oceans of data like it was bathwater, wrote programs in now-extinct dialects of computer language, and conjured a mathematically sound model of the Earth's shape so accurate, your iPhone still thanks her every time it finds the nearest gas station.

Let's be clear: she did this in an environment about as welcoming as a cactus in a boardroom. One of only a handful of Black employees. A woman, in a place where "women in science" was still filed under science fiction. And yet, she *did the math*. Not metaphorically; literally. She did the math that allowed satellites to navigate Earth's messy geometry with pinpoint precision—without which GPS would be like trying to use a sundial in a thunderstorm.

Yes, others had their hands in the celestial cookie jar—military minds like Bradford Parkinson pushed the project forward with Cold War zeal, and physicists like Ivan Getting dreamed of space-based location systems before "space-based" was a thing people said without giggling.

But none of them had to mold the very planet like digital clay. None of them stared into punch cards and thought, "This is how we fix the problem of knowing where the hell we are."

So next time your GPS reroutes you after you miss a turn, spare a thought for Dr. West. And maybe whisper a quiet apology to the machine, too: it's working hard, spinning equations on a model built by a woman most people still haven't heard of, who gave us the gift of not being utterly, totally, tragically lost.

And that, in a world that still forgets its heroes, is about as close to poetry as math ever gets. It even rhymes: *Gladys West, GPS.*

— Further Reading —
West, Gladys B., *It Began With A Dream*. Igwest Publishing, 2020.

Chapter 43 Therac-25

The story of the Therac-25 is an exemplar of a distinctly modern kind of disaster: one in which human error is so meticulously transcribed into code that it becomes systemic, invisible, and lethally efficient. Unlike the bridge collapses and mine explosions of yesteryear, which at least had the theatrical courtesy to announce themselves with groaning steel and falling masonry, the Therac-25's destruction unfolded mostly in clinical silence, behind hospital doors, under the soothing hum of a machine designed to heal.

Developed by Atomic Energy of Canada Limited, the Therac-25 was the product of that particularly dangerous genre of institutional thinking in which technological innovation is pursued with more enthusiasm than scrutiny. It was a medical linear accelerator, meant to deliver precise doses of radiation to cancer patients. It also, owing to a catastrophic software bug, delivered lethal overdoses with an efficiency that would have impressed Dr. Strangelove.

The failure itself was an instructive masterpiece of compounded error. In an effort to streamline the device, engineers removed hardware safety interlocks, assuming, optimistically, that the software would pick up the slack. The software, however, contained a *race condition*: a term that, in programming circles, describes a scenario where multiple processes compete in a way that produces unpredictable and unintended results. In this case, "unintended" is putting it mildly. If an operator entered commands too quickly—a scenario as inevitable as gravity—the machine could misfire, delivering hundreds of times the intended radiation dose while politely insisting that nothing was wrong.

The results were, predictably, horrifying. Patients, expecting targeted radiation therapy, found themselves on the receiving end of doses more appropriate for nuclear accident sites. Some reported immediate searing pain. Others suffered burns so deep they reached bone, accompanied by a frying sound from the machine, though to be normal, and explained away as "saturated ion chambers" in the Therac device.[20] A number of them died, not from their original illness, but from the treatment itself: medical tragedy reimagined as dystopian farce.

One might assume that such an egregious failure would lead to swift corrective action. One would be wrong. The initial response from the manufacturer involved the usual corporate sophistry, including the ever-reliable "operator error" defense, a phrase that, in this instance, functioned more as an incantation against liability than a meaningful explanation. Only after multiple fatalities and sustained external scrutiny did the company acknowledge that, in fact, their supposedly infallible software had all the reliability of a rigged roulette wheel.

The Therac-25 debacle is now an obligatory case study in engineering ethics, though one suspects that its lessons—chief among them, that blind faith in software is indistinguishable from negligence—are learned only briefly before being discarded in the next wave of technological hubris. It is a reminder that complexity, far from guaranteeing sophistication, often masks its own lurking hazards. And that, as history shows with unnerving consistency, no machine is more dangerous than one designed by people who refuse to believe it can fail.

— Further Reading —

Perrow, Charles, *Normal Accidents: Living with High-Risk Technologies*. Princeton University Press, 1984.

Leveson, Nancy G., *Safeware: System Safety and Computers*. Addison-Wesley, 1995.

Chapter 44 Shuttle Challenger

The day the Challenger was destroyed was not merely an accident. It was the consequence of years of the institutional complacency and bureaucratic brinkmanship that had built up to this time. It was indeed the end of a long and complex decision-making process, wherein politics, PR, and the grinding inertia of mammoth organizations twist and transform an engineering hiccup into a national catastrophe.

NASA, having once represented the pinnacle of rationalism and scientific progress, had by the mid-1980s acquired a troubling secondary function: public spectacle. The shuttle program, pitched as the dawning of an era in which spaceflight would be as routine as commercial air travel, was in reality a system riddled with technical compromises and political expediency. The illusion of safety, carefully maintained by a string of previous successes, was finally punctured by an unsparing reality: a piece of rubber, subjected to subfreezing temperatures, had lost its flexibility, and in so doing, had sealed the fate of seven astronauts.

The O-ring failure was, in purely mechanical terms, almost mundane. A minor seal, one of thousands of components on the shuttle, ceased to function correctly, allowing superheated gases to escape and burn through the external fuel tank. But what elevates the Challenger disaster from mere technological mishap to a case study in the perils of human decision-making is that the failure was both predictable and preventable. Engineers at Morton Thiokol, acutely aware of the risks, had warned NASA officials in no uncertain terms. The response from NASA was not merely indifference; it was active dismissal. Managers, under pressure to meet schedules that had more to do with political optics than engineering prudence, overrode the objections. The decision to launch was made not on the basis of science, but on the assumption that past success was an indicator of future safety: a logical fallacy of such breathtaking negligence that it should be studied alongside TV psychics, Scientology, and the aforementioned Therac-25.

The public aftermath followed a familiar script. A commission was convened, testimony was given, and findings were issued in language designed to sound authoritative while diffusing accountability. That the Rogers Commission included figures like Neil Armstrong and Richard Feynman lent it gravitas, but it was Feynman, the eternal dissenter, who cut through the bureaucratic fog with a single televised demonstration: an O-ring, placed in a glass of ice water, becoming brittle before the nation's eyes. However, the failure had been too elementary to consider for more than a few seconds. It escaped or was ignored by one of the most sophisticated organizations on earth. The Challenger disaster did not end the shuttle program but irrevocably changed public perception. NASA was once perched on a pedestal of scientific rigor; now it was seen as nothing more than another government agency, whose institutional blindness and rationalized recklessness closely resembled that of any other bureaucracy.

The event remains a stark reminder that technological progress, for all its grandeur, is always at the mercy of those who administer it. The laws of physics are not susceptible to wishful thinking, and no amount of institutional prestige can compensate for a failure to acknowledge reality.

— **Further Reading** —

Feynman, Richard P., *"What Do You Care What Other People Think?": Further Adventures of a Curious Character*. W.W. Norton & Company, 1988.

— **Easy Viewing** —

Very short video of Feynman demonstrating the O-ring problem: www.youtube.com/watch?v=6Rwcbsn19c0

Chapter 45 The Great Balloonfest Fiasco

For reasons that can only be attributed to unchecked civic enthusiasm and an underdeveloped understanding of meteorology, the city of Cleveland in 1986 attempted to set a world record by releasing 1.5 million helium balloons. If you have ever wondered what happens when a small army of well-intentioned Midwesterners weaponizes the laws of physics, the answer is: nothing good.[21]

The plan was breathtaking in its simplicity, which is a polite way of saying that it did not appear to have been thought through. Some 2,500 volunteers were given the task of inflating the balloons, corralled beneath an enormous net that was stretched across a public square like the world's least effective safety measure. When the big moment arrived, the net was released, and the balloons surged skyward initially seeming like a stunning and benign display of whimsical excess. There was cheering. There was a sense of civic accomplishment. And then, rather abruptly, there was a crisis.

A cold front swept in, and instead of dispersing like a flock of helium-filled doves ascending to some metaphorical higher plane, the balloons were shoved back down toward the city like a particularly determined act of meteorological vengeance. Suddenly, Cleveland found itself the unwilling host of a balloon-based apocalypse.

The local airport had to shut down because its runways had transformed into an impromptu ball pit. Highways became choked with what looked like the aftermath of a circus supply truck explosion. But most distressingly, Lake Erie, a place that was never meant to resemble a mid-grade amusement park attraction, was now blanketed in an impenetrable layer of bobbing balloons. This turned out to be a catastrophic problem for the search-and-rescue teams attempting to locate two missing fishermen, since the usual method of spotting a person in distress involves identifying things like movement and contrast: two things not terribly compatible with a lake now indistinguishable from the set of a particularly unsettling children's show.

By the time the search teams were able to navigate the balloon-riddled lake, the missing boaters were found drowned. This was the moment when an innocent record-breaking attempt officially entered the annals of public relations disasters. What had been meant as a lighthearted stunt was now an accidental case study in unintended consequences.

The aftermath was about what you'd expect: lawsuits, finger-pointing, and the general sense that Cleveland had, perhaps, flown a little too close to the sun, except instead of wax wings they had 1.5 million rubber balloons.

— **Easy Viewing** —

See a short video here:

www.youtube.com/watch?v=IR7NqyqxNQs

Chapter 46 The Kegworth Air Disaster

On 8 January 1989, a British Midland Boeing 737-400 with 118 passengers crashed on a highway near Kegworth village in central England. This is a story with both grief and some measure of wisdom, because, as one might imagine, we learned important lessons and applied them to future pilot training.

It began with a minor malfunction: a rattling noise out of one of the engines. But which one?

Both pilots had flown thousands of hours in commercial jets; but fewer than a hundred hours in the new 737-400 models. So they heard that noisy engine and smelled smoke, but pilots can't see the engines from the cockpit. Based on the fact that they could smell smoke, they figured it must be the right engine, because 737s have their cabin intake vents on that side, so they shut down that engine. The rattling stopped.

What they were not trained for was the fact that cabin air in the new "400" version 737s is drawn from both sides.

A plane like that can fly with just one engine, but prudence calls for a reroute and emergency landing. They had been given clearance to head to East Midlands Airport which was nearby. During the approach they mistakenly gave more throttle to the *malfunctioning* left engine, which quickly burst into flames. By then, the right engine couldn't be restarted because it was flying too slowly.

The jet aircraft was now a glider, with no engine power, and not enough altitude to make it to the runway, so it was inevitable it would crash somewhere.

That "somewhere" was the M1 motorway, packed with traffic. The crash killed 47 and injured 74.

However, this disaster taught an important lesson. The incident resulted in a series of profound changes in aviation. The notion of "human factors training" was introduced to the industry: training focused not so much just on the controls and instruments, but on how pilots think and act under stressful situations.[22]

Chapter 47 A Chip with a Big Bug

A Tiny Flaw, a Billion-Dollar Mistake

In 1993, Intel, the global juggernaut of microprocessors, which had made well over a gazillion dollars by convincing the world that its chips could solve the world's most complex problems with effortless precision, suddenly found itself in a rather embarrassing position: It had sold a $300 processor that could do math, *but with errors*. We're talking floating-point division, the kind of calculation that happens in everything from your spreadsheets to NASA's calculations on Mars rovers. This, of course, was a catastrophic oversight, but Intel took its sweet time admitting it.

The bug had one simple consequence: The processor, when tasked with specific types of floating-point operations, would spit out the wrong results, potentially derailing entire projects, misleading stock market predictions, or ruining someone's attempt to finish their high school math homework.[i] Imagine buying an expensive car only to find it randomly stops working while you're on a mountain pass: your hair might stand up, your palms might sweat. The same thing happened here, but on a global scale.[23]

Intel's response to the whole debacle was something you might call "classically corporate." They initially downplayed the severity of the issue, claiming that it was really only an "edge case," one of those rare, hard-to-reproduce problems that didn't matter to 99.9% of users. Of course, in the real world, that's like saying, "Sure, our plane can't take off, but we'll just fly 99% of the time!" Their initial, half-hearted attempts to brush it off were swiftly met with derision from the tech community. Because when you're in the business of making things that do math for people, it's a bad look when your product fails to add two plus two correctly.

---

[i] The error occurred only in floating-point division; even then, only for specific rare inputs. Most typical consumer or business uses would never trigger it.

The result? Intel, the colossus of computer chips, was forced to offer replacements to any customer who asked—a massive reversal from its earlier stance, and a logistical nightmare. The irony? It all happened after the company had spent years marketing itself as the flawless beacon of technological progress, and there they were, grappling with a problem that many would expect from a much smaller, less established company.

Now, when you think of tech giants, the first thing you think of is impeccable reliability. But no, Intel was scrambling to fix their blunder as quickly as possible, offering promises of immediate upgrades. They issued a statement, full of apologies and assurances, as they sought to mend their reputation. But the stain was there, undeniable, like a coffee spill on an expensive suit. Intel had made an error in the most embarrassing way possible: a moment of technological hubris followed by a spectacular reality crash.

You'd think this would have been the end of Intel's world; after all, we were talking about a global meltdown, and that kind of thing could put a company out of business, right? But no. In the grand tradition of corporate America, they weathered the storm, as all companies do. By 1995, the Pentium bug was a footnote in tech history, and Intel was back in business, bigger than ever. But it was a reminder to all of us: Even the most meticulous minds sometimes miss the simplest, most obvious mistakes.

And that, my friends, is how you fail spectacularly in front of the entire world, and live to tell the tale.

— **Further Reading** —
Pratt, Vaughan, "Anatomy of the Pentium Bug," *Stanford University*, Dept. of Computer Science. July 26, 2005.
www5.in.tum.de/~huckle/anapentium

Chapter 48 The Sampoong Department Store Collapse

Tragedy Beneath the Surface of Commerce

The Sampoong Department Store was meant to be a beacon of modern commerce. Instead, it became the gravestone of an unregulated economic philosophy that assumes the free market can, with the grace of an invisible hand, substitute for basic physics. It did not, and on June 29, 1995, the edifice proved itself a spectacularly inefficient support for the people it was meant to serve. It collapsed, unceremoniously and with terrifying speed, into a heap of shattered concrete and broken bodies.

The problem, of course, was not engineering. The mathematics of construction have long been settled; architects know how to keep buildings upright. The problem was the well-documented and thoroughly predictable tendency of human beings to prioritize short-term economic gain over long-term stability. Originally intended as an office building, Sampoong was reimagined—by people with neither the expertise nor the inclination to care—as a high-traffic shopping center. When engineers, those irritating sentinels of reality, objected, they were dismissed. To make room for escalators, several support columns were removed from the design, and others were shaved down, thinner than specified, without compensating reinforcement. Heavy rooftop machinery was shifted in ways that would make any competent designer recoil; and, in a final act of breathtaking myopia, an entire extra floor was added to maximize retail space. The top floor in the approved building plan was to be a relatively light roller rink, but a restaurant was built instead, being much heavier. One might forgive such decisions if they were made in an era when the laws of physics were but vague conjectures, but this was the late 20th century. One did not need the insights of Newton, Euler, or common sense to see what was coming.[24]

And yet, even when the consequences became increasingly difficult to ignore: cracks forming in the walls, ominous sounds echoing through the structure, management remained undeterred. The reason? The same force that has undone empires and bankrupted civilizations: the unwillingness of those in power to acknowledge that their authority does not extend to the physical universe. When the roof caved in and the building collapsed in a grotesque display of cascading failure, it was not simply the materials that gave way; it was the illusion that commercial ambition, unrestrained and unsupervised, could ever be a substitute for expertise.

The lesson of Sampoong is one we are doomed to repeat: wealth and arrogance do not constitute structural integrity. Nor does profit motive act as a replacement for sound engineering. The tragedy was not just that people died,[j] but that they died in precisely the manner that every competent observer could have foreseen, had they been permitted to intervene. The only mystery left to ponder is how many times such a lesson must be taught before it is finally learned.

— **Easy Viewing** —
National Geographic UK, "Why did the Sampoong Department Store Collapse?" www.youtube.com/watch?v=f9bKPdW5pK4

---

[j] 502 people died and about 1,000 were injured.

Chapter 49 Columbia Disaster

NASA Finally Learns a Lesson?

The destruction of the space shuttle Columbia was less a singular catastrophe than the inevitable consequence of a long, slow corrosion. Bureaucratic inertia, managerial arrogance, and a studied indifference to physics conspired to produce a tragedy that was, by any reasonable metric, entirely avoidable. It was not a crisis of technology, but of managerial culture: an organization so accustomed to its own dysfunction that it had begun treating acts of luck as evidence of competence.

For years, NASA had known that foam insulation regularly detached from the shuttle's external fuel tank, striking the orbiter at launch speeds that could, in theory, breach its thermal protection system. That this never resulted in immediate disaster was interpreted not as a warning sign, but as tacit proof that everything was fine. The damage, after all, had never produced an explosion, so it could not be serious. It was an argument less befitting a scientific institution than a gambler at a roulette table who, having won several bets in a row, assumes the laws of probability no longer apply.

This is how Columbia's fate was sealed, not in the final moments of reentry, but years earlier: through a slow, methodical process of dismissing concerns, sidelining engineers, and mistaking routine luck for safety.

Even in orbit, as engineers on the ground quietly panicked over the possibility that the left wing had been compromised, NASA's upper management dismissed the idea of investigating further. A proposal to use classified military satellites to inspect the shuttle for damage was waved off as unnecessary. A rescue mission, however improbable, was not even modeled as a thought experiment. There was, after all, nothing to be done. Better to assume the best and carry on.

And so, on February 1, 2003, Columbia was left to meet its entirely foreseeable end. As it reentered the atmosphere, a jet of plasma surged into the damaged wing, tearing apart its structure in real time. The failure was swift, absolute, and performed for an audience of millions. Within minutes, Columbia had ceased to exist as a spacecraft, reduced instead to a scattering of burning wreckage across the American South.

What remained was the grim postmortem, filled with the usual hand-wringing, congressional hearings, and vows that such a thing would never happen again, exactly as had been said after Challenger. In its official report, NASA would concede that the disaster was not a function of random misfortune but of an institutional pathology: an organization that had come to mistake wishful thinking for engineering.

The most unnerving part of the Columbia tragedy is not that it happened, but that it was allowed to happen. That a space agency, ostensibly dedicated to logic and precision, had, over time, trained itself to ignore basic cause-and-effect relationships. It is an unsettling truth, but one well worth noting: the universe does not need to conspire against us. When sufficiently determined, we are more than capable of engineering our own destruction.

— Further Reading—
NASA, "Columbia Crew Survival Investigation Report." NASA/SP-2008-565, December 30, 2008.
   www.nasa.gov/wp-content/uploads/2015/01/298870main_sp-2008-565.pdf

— Easy Viewing —
Disaster Breakdown, "What Happened To Space Shuttle Columbia." www.youtube.com/watch?v=be711x3s0zM

Chapter 50 Titan Submersible

It has been said (though perhaps not often enough) that nature is a grand old schoolmarm with a hickory stick, and she does not take kindly to those who skip their lessons. The *Titan* submersible, a contraption of dubious construction and excessive optimism, was sent down to the bottom of the Atlantic in June of 2023 to gawk at the wreck of the *Titanic*, and it never came back up. It was not a mystery, nor an act of fate, nor an unfortunate accident. It was exactly what a person with a lick of sense would expect when one goes gallivanting two miles under the sea in a vessel built like a cigar tube on a budget.

Now, if anybody were to venture into the great, crushing depths of the ocean, one would suppose he might first consult those stuffy old experts who have spent their lives wrestling with the disagreeable nature of physics and pressure. But no, that would be too much trouble, and besides, there is nothing so unpopular with a visionary as a fellow with practical knowledge. The makers of the *Titan*, being the kind of men who believe rules are only for the poor and the unimaginative, were warned by every seasoned submariner and engineer worth his salt that their vessel was not fit for the journey. And what did they do? They scoffed, they sneered, and they went ahead anyway, as if the Atlantic Ocean had ever been persuaded by a confident smirk.

The *Titan* was built from carbon fiber—a material about as suited for deep-sea diving as a silk parasol in a hurricane. Its pilot steered with a game controller, which, I daresay, was better suited for pretending to be a submarine than actually being inside one. Safety measures were regarded with the same enthusiasm a cat has for a bath. And yet, people paid a small fortune for the privilege of climbing into this tin can, because nothing attracts the wealthy quite like the promise of being in exclusive danger.

Down it went, and then... well, it didn't come back up. The laws of physics, having been rudely ignored, took their revenge with a swiftness and thoroughness that would be admirable if it weren't so grim. The *Titan* imploded in the blink of an eye, its occupants reduced to legend before they had time to regret their decisions. And then came the mourners and the analysts and the lamentations, as if this were some unexpected tragedy, rather than the most predictable thing since a rooster's crow.

It is a peculiar thing about humankind: we admire courage, but we reward folly just as often. The *Titanic* was felled by arrogance, and now, more than a century later, men have gone to pay their respects by repeating the mistake. There is, I suppose, a lesson in that—but I expect it will be ignored by the next batch of visionaries eager to test the patience of the ocean.

How Could It Have Been Avoided?

Using Certified Materials. Most deep-sea submersibles use titanium or steel, which have been proven to handle high pressure. Carbon fiber was an experimental choice that wasn't properly tested for repeated deep dives.

Following Industry Safety Standards. The Titan was never officially certified by organizations that regulate submarines. If OceanGate had followed proper safety guidelines, the weaknesses in its design might have been caught earlier.

Listening to Experts. Engineers and deep-sea exploration professionals warned OceanGate for years that the Titan's design was unsafe. The company ignored these warnings.

Regular Hull Testing. Submarines that go deep underwater often have their hulls scanned for tiny cracks that could grow over time. Titan's hull wasn't properly inspected after each dive.

The Takeaway

The Titan tragedy was preventable. Instead of following well-established deep-sea safety practices, OceanGate took shortcuts, which led to a disaster. The lesson? Obvious, one would think. Ignoring safety warnings, especially in extreme environments, can have deadly consequences.

— **Further Reading** —

The Guardian, "'Absolutely shocking': Netflix documentary examines how the Titan sub disaster happened."

www.theguardian.com/film/2025/jun/11/titan-sub-disaster-netflix-documentary

Chapter 51 Here Comes Another Asteroid

Danger, Will Robinson!

There's an asteroid zooming around out there called "2024 YR4." It is one such wonder of the cosmos that evokes thoughts of the immense uncertainty of space. A small asteroid of no more than a few hundred meters across, its intriguing trajectory has drawn attention. The odds of it hitting Earth are quite negligible at the moment, but astronomers remain vigilant even for that slight chance; the impact would see the city wiped out in a split second. It's estimated it will fly by Earth (or, perhaps hit it as we first thought) just before Christmas of 2032.

"*2024 YR4*"? Why didn't they name it *Grinch 2032*?

That was the bad news when it was discovered. Luckily, as astronomers have further refined estimates regarding its trajectory, calculations show that it won't hit the Earth, but there's a faint chance it will actually hit the Moon; which would have no effect on us other than a possibly spectacular video.

Until we gather more data about the impact hazard over months to come, uncertainties will continue to reign. And we'll do so with Earth-bound telescopes, as well as the fantastic James Webb Space Telescope. With more data and precise orbital tracking, collision probabilities with the Moon will be easier to calculate. The remaining uncertainties will drastically shrink, leaving the answer much more unequivocal. It is thus a matter of time, and at least for now, we have that.

And here's more good news. NASA's DART (Double Asteroid Redirection Test) mission has shown that we can indeed alter the trajectory of an asteroid. If it had been necessary, the same could be done by nudging this asteroid slightly off its path with a spacecraft sent on a collision course like they did with DART. This is a very delicate and rapid operation, but the science is pretty much there;

with sufficient time, we can avert such disasters that otherwise look unavoidable.

The premise is simple: intervene early, and you have a very high probability of success; if you intervene late, the asteroid might just be too close for any deflection to matter anymore.

Had 2024 YR4 turned out to be a truly serious threat, we do have the technology to change its course. But it's a matter of doing it in time. We typically have limited time with newly discovered asteroids, and time waits for no one (thank you, Mick and Keith).

The fact that we are having a discussion about the possibility of exactly such an operation is a testament to how far we have grown, how much we have learned about the universe out there, and about ourselves. Yet here we are, standing in a precarious position, watching, measuring, and hoping that the odds remain in our favor for all asteroids yet undiscovered. For however far we have come, we find ourselves still but a mere grain of dust in an infinite, chaotic galactic ocean. And that alone is rather humbling.

As of this writing (June 2025), concerns about a potential Earth impact have completely been ruled out. However, the chance of it colliding with the Moon on December 22, 2032 is about 4%, which would be interesting, at any rate.

Part 3 - Collaborations and Rivals

If there's one thing we can learn from the past, it's that collaboration is never as easy as it sounds, and rivalry is never as simple as we think. Sure, it's nice in theory to put two people with great minds in a room and let them create something beautiful, but reality has a funny way of mucking that up. Sometimes, they come out with a triumph; other times, they come out with a mess and a lot of hurt feelings. Occasionally, they both leave wondering how they ended up in the same room to begin with. Rivalries, on the other hand, can be a real spectacle. Think of them as the high-stakes game where no one plays by the rules, and no one leaves without a few bruises. Yet, more often than we care to admit, it's those bruises that give us the greatest innovations and ideas. A little animosity can go a long way, especially when the stakes are high, and the egos involved are even higher.

But then you get the cases where the collaboration's not just about cooperation, it's about survival. Or, in some cases, proving a point: dragging your rival to the table just to show them how much better you are at what you do. Or vice versa. Sometimes, these situations don't so much end as they do explode in fits of success and failure. What we have here, then, is a fascinating and often absurd parade of individuals and partnerships where, in the grand scheme of things, we can't help but marvel at the intricacies of human nature: pride, pettiness, ambition, loss, sorrow, and inspiration, all swirling together to create something far more complicated, and perhaps more meaningful, than anyone could have expected.

Chapter 52 Murdoch & Trevithick

The Unsung Architects of Steam Power

The Industrial Revolution didn't just *happen* like a fistfight at a hockey game, nor was it simply the product of a few agile, over-educated eggheads in lab coats. This great upheaval, rather, came about as somewhere along the line an intellectual traffic-jam had occurred when ideas piled up against one another, some clashing together, others exploding with spectacular results. And right in all that chaos stood two unheralded yet most important men at the inception of steam power: William Murdoch and Richard Trevithick.

Murdoch was the Scotsman whose mind quietly developed ideas, almost apologetically, under the overshadowing presence of James Watt at Boulton & Watt. While Watt grabbed public attention and received much credit by stamping his loud image over all successful developments in the steam engine, Murdoch, who had done his share of important work in the background, now quietly fashioned a high-pressure steam engine. In the 1780s, he built a self-propelled steam carriage that would have brought him into greater prominence-the world having paid no attention. But no history is a fickle beast; its biased interest is specifically toward the boisterous and never toward the subtle. Murdoch has, therefore, slipped into the shadowy regions of history.

In came Richard Trevithick, the Cornishman who decided, unlike Murdoch, that he would not merely be a footnote in someone else's great story. Trevithick was not going to be content like Murdoch by holding himself in the shadows of others. He didn't just make the best mouse trap; he built the first working steam locomotive in 1804. Too bad, though, because the world wasn't ready for his vision; industrialists couldn't quite wrap their heads around it. They needed a few decades to catch up.

"Trevithick and Murdoch"? They never formed a formal partnership, though their professional dance was unmistakable; sometimes synchronized, more often a bit too competitive. Murdoch's loyalty to

Watt and the old guard prevented him from fully supporting Trevithick's radical designs. But there's a quiet, almost conspiratorial sense that Murdoch's innovations in steam power weren't just passive ideas floating around: they may very well have influenced Trevithick's own breakthrough, whether the historians want to admit it or not.

The cruel irony, of course, is that neither man got their due. And Murdoch, a genius by any other standard, remained a shadow in the history of the steam engine. Trevithick, though bold in engineering, died poor and uncelebrated while the machines he conceived changed the world. Theirs is a tale of genius deferred and ideas advanced: two men who created the future only to have it surpassed by a world too late. The Industrial Revolution was always bad at forgetting its real pioneers.

End result: it's a little like watching a good film in reverse. These two—Murdoch the straight-talking genius, and Trevithick the daring—left their mark on the industrial landscape, but the world at the time could not tell who had left it. They were at the wrong time, both visionaries caught in the gears of an industrial machine often indifferent to their contributions. But the age of steam was also about much more than who built the very first locomotive, it was about the hidden contributions of all those brave enough to think different. We can thank those who pushed the boundaries in places that the mainstream never quite reached.

— Further Reading —

Griffiths, John Charles, *The Third Man: The Life and Times of William Murdoch, 1754–1839, the Inventor of Gas Lighting*. London: André Deutsch, 1992.

Burton, Anthony, *Richard Trevithick: Giant of Steam*. Stroud: Aurum Press, 2002.

Chapter 53 Carnegie v. Rockefeller

Bad v. Bad turned Good v. Good

The competition between Andrew Carnegie and John D. Rockefeller represents one of the few rivalries in American industry that can match the grandeur of their vanity, pride and innate insecurities: *Titan vs. Titan*. It was indeed a battle of egos, empire building, and the irrevocable kind of ambition that characterized the Industrial Revolution in the ageless, smoke-choked ambition of the Gilded Age, where industrial giants reshaped nations with all the subtlety of a locomotive.

The Business Rivalry

At the turn of the 20th century, Carnegie and Rockefeller were not just men of wealth, but the quintessence of wealth itself, immense figures whose commercial reach seemed almost endless. Carnegie, the Scottish immigrant who would become the nation's steel czar, transformed not just steel production but the very face of industrial America. He championed the Bessemer process in America, industrializing steel production at unprecedented scale and efficiency; he did not just create steel, he *defined* steel, and in the very definition of his company, Carnegie Steel, which formed the backbone of the later U.S. Steel Corporation. It controlled an astonishing portion of the American steel industry. It was a combination of engineering triumph and efficiency; yet we might add that it stood, like Rockefeller's empire, as witness to capitalism's ferocity that often turned men into heartless human bulldozers, demanding at every stage to crush anything on its path for profit.

Rockefeller, for his part, was less a man of lofty ideals, or perhaps just a cold-blooded monopolist whose precision in plotting schemes *of genius level* (and Darth Vader levels of compassion and altruism) were worthy of, well, somebody's admiration. Through Standard Oil, he became the undisputed master of oil refining, but his methods? Aggressive and callous. He had conspired with railroads in erecting a web of collusion that granted him an almost supernatural certainty in dictating the market. Any possible competitors? They were obliterated by either being absorbed into his expanding empire or totally destroyed financially. This naturally caught the ire of the government, which in 1911 broke up the Standard Oil behemoth into *34 separate companies*; a deed that could either be celebrated as a triumph for competition or merely the consequence of greedy capitalism as embodied by men like Rockefeller.

Their business rivalry, with all its brutality, was the grim reality of uncontrolled capitalism. Yet this was only a curtain raiser to the acts of that drama: from callous unkindness in business, through to the nobler domain of philanthropy. We thus continue this fascinating tale.

The Philanthropy Rivalry

You see, after these men established a degree of wealth that would make kings in Europe look like street urchins, they began to find new outlets for that wealth. Of course, the charitable work was not simply a Grinch-like spontaneous change of heart, but rather an extension of the very same ambition that put them quickly into the capitalist limelight. It was essentially a contest among titans for the title of "Most Benevolent Billionaire." So they essentially started a game of reverse-Monopoly.

Pass "GO"? Don't collect money, give it away! "Go Directly to Jail" was also something they sidestepped.

Carnegie, crowned by lofty dreams of libraries and universities, wanted to shape the intellectual future of humanity. He gave away about 90% of his wealth, establishing Carnegie Hall and Carnegie Mellon University and funding over 2,500 libraries across the globe. One might argue that, for him, the masses were a great untapped resource; if they could just be educated, they could be molded into something more... useful.

As expected, Rockefeller, ever the competitor, matched Carnegie's educational giving with his own type of philanthropy. But instead of arts and intellectualism, Rockefeller's philanthropy became health-oriented, establishing the Rockefeller Foundation and funding critical medical research. His donations were aimed at fighting diseases like malaria and yellow fever, and his patronage helped found the University of Chicago. In a nutshell, Rockefeller not only wanted to teach, but to heal: the final act of self-preservation.

By the time the smoke of their philanthropic battle began to drift from their shoulders, both men were still keenly aware of their unspoken rivalry. Carnegie cultivated the mind; Rockefeller cultivated the body. Each, in their own way, wanted to carve a permanent mark in history; one through the intellectual victory, the other through the medical victory. They could wear the robe of charity, but neither could wash away the stronghold of competition and ruthlessness that had driven them in their earlier days.

Just as much as their philanthropy was about wealth, their rivalry was about power, influence, and the legacy of two men who understood that, in the end, history would remember them for how much they gave away and not just how much they took.

—Further Reading —

Morris, Charles R., *The Tycoons: How Andrew Carnegie, John D. Rockefeller, Jay Gould, and J.P. Morgan Invented the American Supereconomy*. New York: Times Books, 2010.

Andrew Carnegie in 1878

John D. Rockefeller in 1875

Chapter 54 Charles Rolls & Henry Royce

A legacy that redefined automotive excellence

This is a beautiful picture of two men who redefined a luxury car, not as an afterthought, but, if it's not too far-fetched to say it, almost a mystical human accomplishment: Charles Rolls and Henry Royce, names as much linked with the concept of wealth as with the quiet, mechanical genius that turns humdrum engines into something bordering on the divine.

Rolls was born into a wealthy, influential family and had the very particular distinction of indulging the rather strange hobby of aviation, just four years after the Wrights proved the concept at Kitty Hawk. He was into automobile racing and similar high-risk activities, making him what we might call a running socialite: A race against the wind to fill the hours with perhaps another pointless pursuit of speed? But history would show he surpassed the best of engineers and went well beyond immediate self-gratification. He saw Royce's work immediately. To him, Royce's cars were more than cars. They represented status, sophistication and perhaps most importantly control of transport.

Royce was the antithesis of Rolls when it came to showmanship. If Rolls reveled in the limelight, Royce shunned it with all the fervor of a man who had no interest in such trivialities. Craftsman by instinct and soul, singularly devoted to the ideal of perfection in every line, every curve, every turn of a gear, Royce came from a humble and really grounded background in the reality of working-class Victorian England. His precision designs bordered on obsession, yet this very obsession was what made his cars stand out from the mass production glut of machines of the day.

When Rolls met with early designs made by Royce, a chord was touched within him, a deep understanding that these creations had the potential to rise above their utility as objects to become an entirely new category of being: art in motion, where engineering and grace could meet in the loveliest manner.

It was not about transport. It was all about legacy. Royce's master engineering and Rolls' business acumen combined to create an iconic brand. The resulting cars weren't luxury cars though; they were practical cars. They reflected some sort of intellectual refinement: products of an intellectual meeting of minds from different worlds. The Rolls autos seemed to fly through life on their own, having adventure after adventure, one after the other, while Royce never gave up hope of mechanical perfection. This match was between the rigor of science and the artifice of social stature.

Rolls-Royce rolled vehicles out of their factory that were elegant, but were not mere cars. Instead, they were cultural relics that continue to symbolize the marriage of ambition and engineering to this day. The collaboration of Charles Rolls and Henry Royce was hailed as a superb act of creating, the symbol of man's drive to reach for something that is always ultimately unattainable: perfection itself. "Perfection," so it has been stated, is the worst of all possible goals, since it is unachievable. But, as it turned out, an enduring legacy, far more than the two had as businessmen; they shared that legacy as architects of the modern world.

Just a few years after he began flying, Charles Rolls was killed in a crash when the tail of his aircraft, a "Wright Flyer" model, broke off. He was 32. Henry Royce had better luck, living until the graying age of 70.

— Further Reading —

Van Booy, Simon, *Rolls-Royce Motor Cars: Making a Legend*. ACC Art Books, 2020.

Wegener, Herr Danny, *Rolls-Royce: The Pinnacle of Automotive Luxury*. (Independently published) 2025.

Chapter 55 The Wright Brothers

From Bicycle Mechanics to Aviation Pioneers

Wilbur & Orville Wright are among the greatest inventors ever. And yet, they leave behind something rather unusual in their legacy: a giant human feat without pretense and without brazen publicity. They were much more precise in their methods than that old flying myth had us believe. The Wright brothers were no great dreamers of the age of industrialization, but artisans of an age rapidly passing: one in which experimentation and knowledge were never commodities, but ideals to be pursued.

Wilbur was the great pensive one, an *idea man*.[k] He pondered problems and possibilities without drawing hasty conclusions, in the still and intense manner of someone who has looked over the existing frontiers of human understanding with the humble and selfless desire to extend them. The younger brother, Orville, preferred to put his hands to work, and was more grounded in the application of concrete reason in the discipline of the mechanic. He was an artistic soul who knew too well the work of creation, and did not mind getting his hands dirty with sawdust and oil and grime.

This brotherly intellectual partnership was not simply one of conjoining complementary talents, but a series of hard decisions, a slow, almost agonizing waltz of two highly disciplined minds. One might add that it was their determination and discipline that brought them to the far greater miracle of actually flying a self-propelled, heavier-than-air vehicle.

Consider propellers: this was a radical design, even more so from the Wrights, who came from common backgrounds as bike mechanics, without any formal engineering training. They applied all their analytical discipline to consider propellers as "wings" that would create thrust in a fashion parallel to how a wing creates lift.

---

[k] Like "Billy Blaze" in *Night Shift*, but for *real*, and legendarily so.

Most other inventors at the time were basing their designs off old boat or balloon prop designs; the Wrights saw that something much more efficient and aerodynamic was required.

They took every element of designing propellers very seriously, using the same line of reasoning as for wing design: balancing lift and drag and determining the angles and shapes needed to maximize thrust. They built their own wind tunnel to collect data to test and refine designs. Iterating the blade's shape and pitch with airflow dynamics was something nobody else had considered before, and took hundreds of hours. An efficient source of forward thrust was necessary considering the primitive, heavy engine they used had but 12 horsepower. Many decades later, using computational fluid dynamics and modern analytical tools, engineers evaluated the Wrights' propeller design. The consensus was that their long, funny-looking propeller was about 85% efficient, an astonishing figure given the materials, tools, and primitive workshop they had at their disposal.

Hence the brothers were *more than just efficient*: they were effective. Their propellers smashed their competition out of the park. It was an empirically validated design that was so nearly perfect and uncomplicated that it could be baked into aviation practice like a doughnut: for years a mainstay. That two guys from a bicycle workshop could design and build a propeller with such precision and insight is a testament to their ingenuity and doggedness; and proof that the right mix of intuition, testing and innovation can and should serve as an acid test.

If you think a laboratory is some grand workshop or a corporate think tank for research, think again. A sandy oceanside patch at Kitty Hawk is one part of North Carolina where "experimentation" is less a fancy word than a necessity. They concluded that Ohio's stagnant air wouldn't do the trick, and that the steady winds off the Atlantic might give their flying machine the push it needed.

They refined their machine with each flight, each failed attempt shaping their eventual triumph like the wind itself sculpted the dunes around them. Yet, even as the Wrights' ingenuity lifted them above the sand, life had its own way of grounding them.

Here lies the disturbing thought: What was left when Wilbur died in 1912 of typhoid fever? Orville had lost his brother, his partner, his collaborator. In essence the Wright brothers became little more than a singularity split in two. Without Wilbur, Orville felt lost. That joy of creating, of testing, of achieving the impossible disappeared; he lost his partner, his best friend. Yet here he was, the only survivor, and the legacy of flight and progress he shared with Wilbur somehow seemed cold and incomplete.

But Orville went on, in spite of the loss. He did sell the Wright Company, and living until the age of 76, he saw the wonders that his work—*their work*—had set in motion: jets soaring across the skies, men walking upon the moon as Dr. Robert Goddard had envisioned around 1915. There is a beautiful cosmic irony in the thought that for all his silence, for all the silence of his brother, for all their unwillingness to carry the burden of "fathers of flight," the Wright brothers have stuck their indelible mark on the world. More than anything, their legacy was the strange and humble fact that they had done it: that, in all their quiet, persistent ways, they had made it happen.

Perhaps you've seen the brilliant (and often hilarious) sci-fi TV show, *The Orville*. Seth MacFarlane explained that he named it after Orville Wright as a tribute to the spirit of exploration and innovation in aviation, and in space travel.[25]

The Wright brothers, who, during their brief time on Earth, accomplished what had been only a dream for mankind for centuries, were never dreamers, at least, not as we imagine them. They were systematic engineers. What was left behind was hardly a legacy of fanciful ideals. They were no gods of the skies; but they were diligent geniuses. In a modest way, just two men who saw birds, and saw automobiles; they flew kites and gliders, and pondered, "What if we put a motor on one of these things?"

Gustave Whitehead

The problem with history is that it insists on being tidy, which is a shame, because reality is a mess. The Wright Brothers get the credit for inventing powered flight, and that's fine, except for the minor detail that Gustave Whitehead *may have* beaten them to it. But history has a way of treating inconvenient pioneers the way a dog treats homework: thoroughly chewed up and largely forgotten.

Whitehead, a German immigrant with an impressive mustache and an even more impressive disregard for physics as other people understood it, supposedly got a powered plane off the ground in 1901, in Bridgeport, Connecticut. No Orville, no Wilbur; just a man, his machine, and the kind of audacity that, had things gone differently, might have put his face on a cereal box. His aircraft, *No. 21*, was reportedly a lovely contraption, with bat-like wings and a rotary engine that wouldn't have looked out of place in a Jules Verne fever dream. It ran on kerosene, a fine choice if your goal is to smell like a malfunctioning oil refinery, but also a remarkably modern innovation.

Yet, Whitehead's claim remains murky. No surviving aircraft. No definitive photos of his flights. Just some witness accounts, a handful of newspaper reports, pictures of his gliders and his engine, and a lingering suspicion that history isn't as settled as the Wright estate might prefer. Speaking of which: did you know the Smithsonian has a contract that essentially forbids the museum from even entertaining the idea that Whitehead got there first? In 1948, they signed an agreement with the Wright family stating, in effect, that if they so much as *suggest* another claimant to the throne of powered flight, they'll have to return the original Wright Flyer. Because nothing says "scientific integrity" like a legally binding historical gag order.[26]

So, did Whitehead fly first? Maybe. Maybe not. If there's one thing the Wright Brothers had that Whitehead didn't, it wasn't just powered flight—it was a good lawyer. This doesn't negate the brilliance and steadfast work of those relentless brothers, but Whitehead is an interesting wrinkle to this whole tale.

— Further Reading—
McCullough, David, *The Wright Brothers.* Simon & Schuster, 2016.

Orville (R) and Wilbur (L), 1909

Chapter 56 Curtiss-Wright

From Patent Battles to Shared Skies

Human flight itself was not a smooth climb but a contest of intellect and ambition. The Wright brothers and Glenn Curtiss were more than competitors. They were ideological rivals in an aerial arms race engaged in years of litigation over the essence of controlled flight. The feud, though fueled by technical genius, became a tyrannical obstacle to American aviation.

The Wright brothers received a patent in 1906 for their wing-warping control system, which they claimed to be the foundation of all practical aviation. Its legal argument was broad: it claimed dominion over a method and over aerodynamic control in general. In his own way, Glenn Curtiss adapted the problem by using ailerons, much smaller flaps on wing that controlled airflow without bending the wings. Curtiss' design was, in fact, far superior. The Wrights, though, didn't recognize the difference between means and ends: They said Curtiss invaded their intellectual property. So in 1909 the courtroom became an extension of their battle for intellectual domination. Injunctions and legal maneuvers took the place of the gears and rivets of aviation.

The results were dire. Lengthy legal hostilies overshadowed American aviation and discouraged investment and innovation. The fear of litigation became as formidable a hindrance as the laws themselves. The world was getting closer to an era in which air supremacy would define military might, and the American aviation industry was stuck in courtroom bureaucracy rather than flying across new frontiers.

But time is the ultimate arbitrator. In 1912, as we know, Wilbur Wright died leaving Orville to fight alone. By 1914 the struggle had paid its price. By 1915, Orville had sold the Wright Company, grown weary of the struggle, and left aviation behind. But the tale was by no means over when Orville left town. Whatever remained of the Wright organization merged with Curtiss's company to become the Curtiss-Wright Corporation by 1929. And this merger was blessed with ill luck: it was near the center of the Great Stock Market Crash and the Great Depression.

One of aviation history's giants emerged from that unwilling union. Curtiss-Wright was among the founding fathers of army aviation, providing airplanes, props and engines to combatants in several of the most epic aerial battles of the twentieth century. Though not personally involved in the merger, Orville lived to see his name snagged by that of his rival; quite poetic, really, to end the bitter dawn of flight.

Curtiss-Wright lives on, a vestige of a corporate war where the sky was more than a frontier: it was a battleground for ingenuity and ambition. Their story of rivalry and synthesis reflects the paradox of progress: that an obstructive clash of great minds can still feed the engines of history in the end.

— **Further Reading** —
Goldstone, Lawrence, *Birdmen: The Wright Brothers, Glenn Curtiss, and the Battle to Control the Skies*. Ballantine Books, 2014.

A Curtiss-Wright Travel Air CW-12Q

Chapter 57 Max Valier & Fritz von Opel

Rocket men before rockets ruled the sky

The late 1920s were a heady time for technological ambition, with aviation still proving that gravity was more of a suggestion than a law, and automobiles rapidly evolving from sputtering deathtraps into slightly more elegant, high-speed deathtraps. Enter Max Valier and Fritz von Opel, two men who, upon considering the miracle of combustion engines, decided they weren't quite combustible enough. Their solution? Rocket propulsion, naturally.

Now, any rational person might pause before the idea of bolting explosive canisters onto the back of a car, but Valier and von Opel were undeterred by such pedestrian concerns as "structural integrity" and "not dying in a fireball." Their project, part mad science and part industrial-scale pyromania, saw automobiles hurtling forward in bursts of barely controlled chaos. There were no seat belts, no crash tests, and certainly no liability waivers. What there was, however, was an ample supply of things that could *and did* go wrong.

Max Valier, in particular, was a man whose enthusiasm far exceeded his life expectancy. His fate, while tragic, was also somewhat inevitable: in 1930, one of his experimental rocket engines opted for a more immediate and violent form of deconstruction, taking him with it. Fritz von Opel, presumably realizing that he'd now inherited both the future of rocket travel and the distinct possibility of his own obituary, promptly reconsidered his career choices. The dream of the rocket car fizzled out, not with a whimper, but with an exceptionally large bang.

To this day, the notion of strapping high-powered explosives to vehicles remains, mercifully, the domain of stunt drivers and exceptionally misguided inventors. Yet, in a way, Valier and von Opel did pave the way for a certain kind of progress, demonstrating that just because something is technically possible doesn't mean you should actually do it.

— **Further Reading** —

Neufeld, Michael J., *The Rocket and the Reich*. Smithsonian Books, 2013.

Hagerty, Jack, and Rogers, Jon C., *Spaceship Handbook*. ARA Press, 2001.

Chapter 58 Flaky Corn

Health fanatic, inventor, and breakfast icon

In the wild and wacky world of 1890s Michigan, a *medical doctor* actually convinced people that the road to heavenly salvation ran directly through their digestive tracts.

Dr. John Harvey Kellogg, a mustachioed health guru with the intensity of a caffeinated squirrel and the libido of a neutered chess piece, ran the Battle Creek Sanitarium, where America's constipated elite paid good money to have yogurt enemas shot up their fancy backsides. (These were considered the "good old days," which I hasten to add, included separate water fountains and women not yet voting.)

Meanwhile, his brother Will stood by watching John's food experiments with mounting horror and occasional mathematical calculations. Then one day, through a hilarious kitchen screw-up that would today involve someone getting fired and possibly sued, they accidentally let some wheat go stale, ran it through rollers, and BOOM! The most exciting thing to come out of Battle Creek since boredom itself.

Enter C. W. Post, former sanitarium guest and future breakfast kingpin. Post watched the Kellogg brothers' operation with the same expression your cat has when eyeing your unattended sandwich. Then, in a move combining the subtle grace of a corporate espionage thriller with the ethical standards of a swamp full of piranhas, he started his own cereal company *right down the street.*

The whole situation exploded when Will committed the ultimate betrayal in his brother's eyes: he added SUGAR to the cereal! John might as well have caught Will dancing naked around a pentagram while sacrificing organic vegetables to the devil. Their relationship crumbled faster than off-brand corn flakes in warm milk and thus began perhaps the longest family silent treatment in history.

So there you have it! America's breakfast table: forever transformed by a doctor who thought sex was bad, a businessman who thought profits were good, and a competitor who essentially photocopied their homework and got an A+. Next time you're pouring milk over your morning flakes, remember: you're not just eating cereal, you're consuming the scattered remnants of a bizarre health cult with a side order of family dysfunction. Plus ferric orthophosphate, niacinamide, and riboflavin.

But wait, there's more.

Over the years, Will Keith became more successful, and the two continued their mutual silent treatment. Will was told about odd behavior by John, so he went to Florida to see how his brother was doing. Will Keith was shocked to find that John was losing his grip on reality. John Harvey Kellogg passed away in 1943 at the age of 91. Before he died, he wrote Will Keith a letter to make amends, saying sorry for his actions.

However, Will Keith never received it. He was almost totally blind, and his staff didn't tell him about the letter. Years later, while on *his* deathbed in 1951, Will Keith was finally informed of the letter. Realizing he had missed his brother's apology, he sat up and exclaimed, "Why didn't anyone tell me this sooner?" And he wept.

— Further Reading —

Markel, Howard, *The Kelloggs: The Battling Brothers of Battle Creek*. Vintage, 2018.

Chapter 59 Laurel and Hardy

More than just another fine mess

Laurel and Hardy were comedians cut from entirely different cloths. They were the gravitational pull in a unique universe where the rest of the galaxies somehow orbited slapstick, the absurd, and exquisite frustration. To call them a "duo" is akin to calling the Pacific Ocean "some water": technically correct but insufficiently grand. They didn't act; they executed comedy with the kind of precision that suggests either divine intervention or a great deal of time spent accidentally sitting on rakes.

Stan Laurel could have walked down the street with a sign around his neck that read "Questions: open for business." He always seemed to have just walked over from another century and was too polite to tell that it was not his place. In his mind there was a series of large catastrophes building up to some kind of ultimate failure, too much like a man trying to iron his own trousers while wearing them to be anything but funny. Oliver Hardy strolled like an offended duke who just realized his fortune consisted of unpaid bar tabs. There was the world-weary knowledge a man must feel after sending back a steak and getting a plate of wet toast instead, but deep down, he knows it is partly *Stan's* fault.

They cooperated for the first time in a movie entitled *The Lucky Dog* (1921), which almost certainly carries an ironic sense since neither of them ever saw such a thing as luck. By the time their teaming was a fact in the late 1920s, they had already combined their strengths into a bond at atomic level: Laurel's innocence and Hardy's irritation, all of it happening while the cosmos always conspired against them. Of their best movies—*The Music Box* (1932), *Sons of the*

Desert (1933), *Way Out West* (1937) —none were simple comedies; all were scientific studies in entropy, demonstrating what happens when bad luck encounters very simple tasks (moving a piano, for example).

Yet even with all that, they floundered in the dangerous waters of the early Hollywood market. The studio system, a well-oiled machine specifically designed to convert talent into profit while ensuring as little of that profit as possible reached the talent, kept them on a financial leash. Hal Roach, their studio head, paid them well enough to keep them working but not so well that they could ever leave. One suspects that if Roach had been put in charge of gravity, he would have found a way to charge people for falling down. Hardy's alimony payments to his ex-wife, and his love of gambling added to his financial problems.

As the years wore on, so did their luck, unraveling not with a bang but with the long, slow wheeze of a joy buzzer running out of energy. By the 1940s, comedy had evolved; or at least changed suits. Verbal jousts and fast-talking dames had shoved aside the silent stumble and the perfectly timed toe-stomp and pie to the face. Laurel and Hardy, whose stock-in-trade was calamity conducted like a symphony, suddenly found themselves looking like two well-meaning vaudevillians who'd stumbled into a cocktail party hosted by Noël Coward. They kept at it, of course; what else could they do? But the timing was off, the costumes didn't quite fit, and the laughter had moved to another room.

Their final film, *Atoll K*, filmed in Europe and apparently written in Esperanto and despair, was an exercise in international misunderstanding. The set was chaotic, the direction vague, the budget cautious to the point of cowardice. Both men were in poor health: Stan was dealing with ulcers and the slow erosion of diabetes; Ollie, meanwhile, was succumbing to the dual hazards of physical comedy and American gravy. It wasn't so much a production as a slow-moving eulogy disguised as a farce.

Hardy's decline was the kind of grim inevitability usually reserved for classical tragedies and poorly made casseroles. A massive stroke silenced him; this, from a man who could express volumes with a raised eyebrow and the slow turn of a head. He died in 1957 at 65, a gentle man deflated by years of pratfalls, comic kismet, and buffet lunches. Laurel was inconsolable in the quiet, understated way of stagebound soulmates who've spent decades perfecting the art of understated chaos. "I'd never perform without him," he said, and he meant it. He retired from the stage, the screen, and any public arena that might mistake his absence for forgetfulness.

Stan Laurel spent his final years in a modest Santa Monica apartment, telephone number listed, door occasionally open to those brave enough to knock. He answered fan letters by hand, often with the same succinct brilliance he once used to undercut Hardy's bluster with a blink. Robin Williams would have hated this final setting, while Truman Capote would have adored it: sunlight, silence, and a man holding court with ghosts. There were no grand farewells, no tributes with brass bands. Just a fading presence, keen-eyed and sardonic, surrounded by a past he didn't need to embellish. He'd lived it once, and that was enough.

When he died in 1965, at 74, it marked the end of a certain kind of laughter; the kind that didn't require cruelty or commentary. Just a banana peel, a bowed head, and a reminder that dignity, when properly fumbled, is the funniest thing in the world.

Yet, history has been kinder to them than Hollywood ever was. They are still studied, still imitated, still beloved. Their influence is baked into everything from *Looney Tunes* to the *Dick van Dyke Show* to *Saturday Night Live*, their legacy proving that true genius doesn't fade, it merely waits for the next generation to rediscover it. They may have left this world with far fewer riches than they deserved, but their wealth was measured in laughter, and that, at least, has proven immune to inflation.

— Further Reading —
McCabe, John, *Laurel & Hardy.* Barnes & Noble, 1996.

Stan Laurel (1930)

Oliver Hardy (1925)

Chapter 60 Vidal v. Buckley

Gore Vidal and William F. Buckley Jr. were like the intellectual equivalent of two bulls locked in a tiny arena, only neither one was willing to back down. Vidal, a sharp-witted iconoclast, tore through America's sacred cows with a kind of glee reserved for those who'd already seen the emperor's nakedness and decided to point it out with sharp, barbed comments. He didn't just criticize; he dissected, finding the soft underbelly of everything he deemed hypocritical, including America itself. Beneath the sarcasm, there was real compassion, a kind of disdain for the system, not out of bitterness, but out of sheer disappointment that it hadn't lived up to the lofty promises of democracy.

Then you had Buckley, the dapper, always-composed spokesperson for a certain brand of elitist conservatism that practically dripped from his perfectly tailored suit. With his elaborate vocabulary and that peculiarly English superiority, Buckley believed himself the keeper of virtue, the one holding the moral compass in a world gone mad. His intellectual pomp seemed to suggest that he was too refined to engage with the rough, gritty edges of the world; that was for others. Reality? Let's just say his grasp of it was... selective.

Buckley actually tried to critique John Lennon's lyrics in "Imagine," thus adding to his reputation as someone who took aim at what he saw as threats to Western civilization, even if those threats were coming in the form of a rock song from one of the most beloved musicians of his time. You know, because, in Buckley's mind, it's ludicrous, even insane, to envision a world of peace and harmony where evidence and reality reign over fantasy and hate.

When Vidal and Buckley met, it was like intellectual fire meets intellectual gasoline: a perfect storm. Their 1968 debate was a legendary moment in television. Buckley, with all the pomp of an aristocrat defending a crumbling empire, tried to wrestle control, but

Vidal, with relentless sarcasm, gave him no quarter. When Buckley, utterly losing his cool, went full-juvenile and flung the word "queer" at Vidal (who was gay), it was as if the intellectual air itself froze. Vidal, cool as ever, shot back with a fearless, cutting rejoinder that was as much an indictment of Buckley's moral certainty as it was a show of Vidal's own superiority: not just as a verbal pugilist, but in every way that defines an adept, unflappable intellectual.

Gore Vidal got so *thoroughly* under Buckley's famously patrician skin that the normally composed conservative lion unraveled on live television, reduced to sputtering *ad hominem*, the last resort of a frustrated bully suddenly aware he's monumentally outmatched. So unhinged was Buckley that he actually *threatened to punch Vidal in the face* on national TV, no less.

That moment, drenched in bravado and intellectual ferocity, marked the bitter edge of their rivalry, a feud that would follow both men in their later years. Yet, it wasn't just the words that carried weight; it was the entire clash of ideologies, the titanic collision of two worldviews that couldn't have been more at odds, yet were bound to interact like opposing forces of nature.

— Easy Viewing —
The legendary Gore Vidal vs. William F. Buckley Jr. exchange:
www.youtube.com/watch?v=MZ1cRbkoPus

Chapter 61 Bill Murray and Chevy Chase

Too cool to get along

Bill Murray and Dan Aykroyd have long been comedy's version of the perfect pair, like two gears in a clock that always mesh seamlessly, never missing a beat. Face it, as loved as they are, they were no Laurel and Hardy, not by a long shot, but they were built for each other, on *Saturday Night Live*, in *Ghostbusters* and beyond, their offbeat humor clicked with the precision of a lock and key. It's not just that they get along; it's that they have a shared rhythm that clicks in ways most comedy duos can only dream of. I can't help but imagine where Dan Aykroyd might have seamlessly fit into *Groundhog Day*, or how Bill Murray might have added even more magic to *Trading Places*.

But then, there's Chevy Chase. If you were to ask anyone who was around in the early days of *SNL*, you'd quickly learn that the Chevy Chase show was, well, the *Chevy Chase* show. Self-assured to a fault, always the center of attention, and prone to tripping over his own ego. Bill Murray didn't take kindly to this; he wasn't interested in competing with the man for the spotlight. As a result, the relationship between Chase and Murray was, how do we say this, *strained*. There were plenty of rough patches, fueled by clashes of personality and comedic styles. Murray, with his deadpan, sardonic wit, had no time for the more bombastic brand of humor by the man with the dimpled chin named after an automobile (and a city in Maryland). If there were two forces in the universe that didn't seem meant to collide, it was these two. Oil and water. Peanut butter and toothpaste. Ozzy Osbourne and the Dalai Lama.

And speaking of the Dalai Lama... we have *Caddyshack*, and things got interesting. This wasn't just a film, it was an ensemble of egos, a cocktail of conflicting comedic minds, where each actor's persona was amplified by the chaos of the set. With Murray and Chase, that chaos was palpable. Their tension wasn't just the stuff of behind-the-scenes gossip; it was front and center, simmering just below the surface, threatening to boil over. And yet, in the oddest way, this tension worked. Both men were brilliant improvisers, and somehow, the energy between them translated into some of the most unforgettable moments in the film.

They never fully reconciled. In fact, it wasn't until the last days of filming that they managed to coexist long enough to finish the movie. Did they reach some heartfelt understanding? Hardly. Was there an awkward handshake and a forced mutual respect? Not so much. But for *Caddyshack* to have succeeded, both men had to put their personal differences aside, if only for the sake of the film. It was like running holy water through a Bass-O-Matic, but the resulting concoction was comedy gold, somewhat akin, instead, to the famed *Mentos and Diet Coke Experiments*.

And so, the story of Bill Murray, Chevy Chase, and an amicable animated rodent became not just about actors overcoming egos, but about how tension, if handled just right, can produce the most unexpected brilliance. Bishop Pickering would give his blessings.

— Further Reading —

Shales, Tom, and Miller, James Andrew, *Live From New York: The Complete, Uncensored History of Saturday Night Live as Told by Its Stars, Writers, and Guests*. Back Bay Books, 2015.

Part 4—Myth and Mystery

Human beings have an impressive ability to ignore reality in favor of something more interesting. Show them a perfectly logical explanation for why boats occasionally disappear near Bermuda, and they'll nod politely before launching into a ten-minute diatribe about alien abductions, interdimensional portals, or an ancient Atlantean curse. The truth is, people don't just enjoy myths; they cling to them like a cat to a screen door, claws dug in, hissing at anyone who dares suggest that, no, the Loch Ness Monster is not a prehistoric reptile that somehow survived for millions of years in a single, moderately-sized lake without anyone ever hitting it with a fishing boat.

And though most of those stories might be as ridiculous as imaginable, they refuse to die since they tickle our imagination with the hope that the world may still hold strange and indescribable things. Maybe St. Patrick really did send all the snakes out of Ireland. Perhaps there's really a giant, tentacled horror lurking at the bottom of the ocean waiting for that perfect moment to snatch a cruise liner. The Chupacabra really exists and is terribly misunderstood; just a lonely bloodsucking cryptid looking for love in all the wrong livestock pens.

In Part 4 of this book, we'll explore these myths with the skepticism they deserve and the enthusiasm they demand, because while they may not be true, they are, at the very least, gloriously entertaining.

Chapter 62 The Tale of Medusa and the Gorgons

If Greek mythology has taught us anything—and let's be clear, it has taught us *many* things, mostly about the perils of accepting unsolicited gifts from gods—it's that being a beautiful woman in ancient Greece was about as safe as being a gazelle in a lion's den. Case in point: Medusa. Once a perfectly ordinary, breathtakingly attractive mortal, she made the unfortunate mistake of existing within range of Poseidon, a deity who spent an alarming amount of time treating human women like a buffet table. When he assaulted her in Athena's temple, the goddess, in a display of logic that suggests Olympians were just making things up as they went along, decided the real problem here wasn't divine misconduct but Medusa's *face*. Solution? Transform her into a scaly, snake-haired horror show whose mere glance could turn a person into a particularly lifelike statue.

Naturally, this ruined her dating prospects. And as if that weren't enough, along came Perseus, a young man whose greatest talent was showing up unprepared and being handed legendary weaponry like a particularly lucky contestant on a game show. Armed with a mirrored shield (to avoid eye contact), a sword he didn't earn, and some winged sandals that, let's be honest, sound like a terrible idea from an ankle support standpoint, he waltzed into Medusa's cave, lopped off her head, and stashed it in a bag like a medieval lunchbox. This was then used as an all-purpose petrification device, because nothing says "hero" like carrying around the severed head of a woman you just murdered.

Medusa after plastic surgery (actual photo)

Over time, Medusa has been rebranded as everything from a cautionary tale about hubris to an ancient feminist icon who just wanted men to leave her alone. The real takeaway, of course, is that mythology is full of moral lessons, most of which boil down to: "The gods are capricious, heroes are freeloaders, and if you find yourself in ancient Greece, it is best to remain deeply unattractive at all times.

Chapter 63 St Patrick

Saint Patrick's life was, by any modern metric, an absolute train wreck. First, he was kidnapped by Irish raiders, which, if we're being honest, is not a great start. Then, after spending six years as a sheep-wrangling prisoner, he managed to escape, only to later return to Ireland voluntarily, because apparently, trauma wasn't enough; he needed closure. His mission was to convert the Irish to Christianity, which, given the spiritual leanings of the time, probably felt a lot like trying to get a room full of toddlers to appreciate tax law.

And then, of course, there's the snake thing. Yes, Saint Patrick is a historical figure, but the snakes? The legend goes that Saint Pattycakes heroically drove all the snakes out of Ireland, which would have been an extraordinary feat if there had been any snakes to begin with. There weren't. Nature had already done the job for him, making his legendary accomplishment about as impressive as announcing that you have successfully removed all the poisonous kangaroos from Iceland. But because humans love a good story more than they love factual accuracy, the tale stuck.

What also stuck, oddly enough, was the global insistence on celebrating Saint Patrick's Day by turning entire cities into questionable shades of green. Chicago, for example, dyes its river so aggressively green that one suspects it could be seen from orbit. Not to be left out, Lithuania follows suit with the Vilnia River, ensuring that no body of water is safe from the enthusiastic application of unnatural food coloring.

And then there are the parades. Every year, people march through city streets, waving Irish flags, wearing absurd amounts of green, and generally behaving as though Saint Patrick's greatest accomplishment was inventing beer. This is a particularly impressive feat of historical rebranding, given that Patrick was, at least in theory, a religious figure, and his modern holiday is best known for encouraging public intoxication at truly reckless levels.

According to the *Catholic Encyclopedia*,[27] "His remains were wrapped in the shroud woven by St. Brigid's own hands [an Irish nun]. The bishops and clergy and faithful people from all parts crowded around his remains to pay due honour to the Father of their Faith... His remains were interred at the chieftain's Dun or Fort two miles from Saul, where in after times arose the cathedral of Down."[28]

If Saint Patrick were alive today, one imagines he would have several pressing questions. Among them: "Why is the river glowing?" "Why is everyone wearing green paper hats?" and "Is this really what I spent my life for?" The answer, of course, is *yes*, because people will find a way to turn even the most pious of legacies into an excuse for a very loud party.

Chapter 64 The Pied Piper of Hamelin

The Pied Piper of Hamelin is one of those stories people love to tell their children without really thinking through the implications. The basic premise is that a mysterious musician shows up, clears a town of its rat problem (which, in 13th-century Europe, is a service that should have earned him at least a knighthood), and then, upon being stiffed on his payment, proceeds to abduct all the children. This raises several urgent questions: Why did a town in 1284 have a working budget for rodent removal but no common sense when it came to paying contractors? Why was this guy walking around in a multi-colored outfit, playing the flute like some kind of medieval busker? And most disturbingly: why did *every single child* decide to follow a strange man out of town without question?

But unlike most fairy tales, this one has a disturbing kernel of truth. Something happened in Hamelin in 1284; something so bad that the town has a whole street where music is still banned, which, when you think about it, is quite possibly the least effective way to prevent future mass child disappearances.[29]

Historians, being the wet blankets they are, insist that the "children" were actually settlers recruited to move eastward, which is a slightly more palatable explanation than "they were all murdered by a lunatic in a cape." Others suggest that disease, war, or something equally medievally awful took them. But regardless of the cause, the fact remains that one day, Hamelin had a lot of children, and the next day, it didn't.

To this day, there is a street, *Bungelosenstrasse*, where music and dancing are officially forbidden, a solemn tribute to the lost children. It is an eerie, silent reminder that some stories, no matter how often they are retold, never lose their ability to unsettle.

This brings us to *The Pied Piper* (1972), in which Donovan, best known for warbling about Mellow Yellow and superheroes at daybreak, plays a possibly supernatural musician in a town filled with people so loathsome that you start to root for the plague. The film, wisely, leans into the horror of the situation, making it clear that when a man dressed like a psychedelic fever dream starts playing the flute, the correct response is to run in the opposite direction.[1]

So, why was he "pied"? Does that mean he was drunk? Well, the go-to source for such information would be, of course, *Fractured Fairy Tales* from the Rocky and Bullwinkle Show. There, we discover that our hero smoked a pipe capable of magically producing various types of pies right from the business end of his tobacco pipe. In particular, his tobacco-leaf pies were so enchanted that anyone who took a bite vanished from the town.

Upon further research we discover that, no, he wasn't drunk, and didn't have a magic pie-manufacturing pipe. *Pied* refers to his multicolored clothing. The word comes from the birds, magpies, which are quite colorful.

Ultimately, the real lesson of the Pied Piper story is this: always pay your musicians, never blindly follow strange men in flamboyant outfits, and if your town has a rat problem so severe that you have to resort to magic, you probably have bigger concerns than an unpaid invoice. And you'd be well-advised not to get your historical information from Rocky and Bullwinkle.

— Easy Listening —
Ingrid Bergman - "The Pied Piper of Hamelin" (radio play)
Part 1 (6 minutes):
  www.youtube.com/watch?v=4AePnU7g558
Part 2 (6 minutes):
  www.youtube.com/watch?v=8Qgz7q7PA8Y

---

[1] By the way, Donovan composed the music for the film.

Chapter 65 The Most Mysterious Manuscript

Imagine spending centuries trying to understand a book that may or may not say anything. Welcome to the ongoing spectacle of the *Voynich Manuscript*, a literary practical joke of galactic proportions, an undeciphered masterpiece of esoteric knowledge that just happens to resemble the scribblings of a sleep-deprived wizard with a broken Rosetta Stone.

The thing is old: older than Columbus, older than the idea of buttons on shirts, and possibly older than common sense. It's packed with lavish illustrations of flora that do not grow, constellations that no self-respecting astronomer would claim, and people who look like they were drawn by someone whose only reference was a particularly drunken night at the pub. The text itself? Forget it. Attempts to decode it (the script the writer used has been dubbed "Voynichese") have resulted in scholars oscillating between exhilaration and despair, usually in the same afternoon. It reads like someone threw Latin, Greek, and a handful of Celtic runes into a blender and pressed "purée."

During World War II, America's finest cryptographers—who spent their days untangling the codes of history's most determined villains—had a go at it. They came away mumbling into their coffee. Was it an unknown language? A secret cipher? A medieval shopping list gone terribly wrong? Even AI models have given it a try, with the latest machine-learning efforts concluding that it's... something.[m]

And let's not forget the parade of past owners, each adding a new layer of confusion. A Holy Roman Emperor once owned it, because apparently even royalty liked a good unsolvable puzzle. A Jesuit priest eventually got hold of it, which seems fitting because if ever a book demanded divine intervention, it's this one. Wilfrid Voynich, the hapless book dealer who gave it his name, must have thought he had the find of a lifetime. Instead, he got a riddle wrapped in a mystery and shoved into an indecipherable manuscript, which, as it turns out, makes for one hell of a conversation piece but a truly useless instruction manual for anything practical.

So here it sits, daring each new generation to crack its code. Maybe it's the medieval equivalent of a prank, the work of a bored monk who thought, "This'll keep them busy." Or maybe, *just maybe*, it contains the deepest secrets of a lost civilization. In any case, if you stare at it long enough, you start to suspect it's staring back.

Want to have some more fun with enigmatic texts? Look up the Rohonc Codex (18th century), Ripley Scrolls (15th century), Nova N 176 (12th century), and the Phaistos Disc (from around 1700 BCE). Enjoy! I'm going to find some more Fractured Fairy Tales on YouTube.

— Further Reading —

Skinner, Stephen, *The Voynich Manuscript: The Complete Edition of the World' Most Mysterious and Esoteric Codex*. Watkins Publishing, 2017.

Brumbaugh, Robert S., *The Most Mysterious Manuscript: The Voynich "Roger Bacon" Cipher Manuscript*. Southern Illinois University Press, 1978.

---

[m] We're pretty sure it's not an ad for Ovaltine.

Chapter 66 The Fountain of Youth

The Fountain of Youth (or, as Vincent LaGuardia Gambini would say, *Fountain of Yute*), immortalized in legend, commercialized in St. Augustine, and possibly inspired by a particularly enthusiastic medieval daydream, has long been one of humanity's more charming delusions. The idea that youth, that most fleeting and fickle of conditions, could be restored by a casual dip in a real-life Hot Tub Time Machine is the sort of hopeful nonsense that has sustained both folklore and the skincare industry for centuries.

Naturally, Juan Ponce de León gets roped into the tale, though history suggests that he spent far less time searching for magic water and far more time being a career conquistador, which in the 16th century was less about chivalry and more about being an armed real estate agent with a tendency to declare that the locals' land was, in fact, now his. Born around 1474 in Spain, Ponce hitched a ride with Columbus in 1493, got a taste for the New World, and eventually became the governor of Puerto Rico. By 1513, he set out to expand Spain's reach and stumbled upon a place that would later be known for retirement homes, theme parks, and dubious alligator-wrangling. He called it *La Florida*—which sounds poetic until you realize he named it after a Christian holiday season "Pascua Florida," making it the colonial equivalent of calling a place "Happy Easter, Yoko."

As for the whole Fountain of Youth business, it appears to be a posthumous PR stunt. The first written suggestion that Ponce was chasing enchanted water came years after his death, courtesy of Spanish historian Gonzalo Fernández de Oviedo, who was not above embellishing for dramatic effect. In reality, Ponce was seeking land, power, and whatever passed for job security in an era where most employment contracts ended in dysentery. The closest he likely got to a supernatural experience was probably an undercooked meal.

Nonetheless, myths have staying power, particularly when there's a gift shop involved. St. Augustine has embraced the legend with the enthusiasm of a city that knows selling tickets to a "Fountain of Youth Archaeological Park" is infinitely more lucrative than inviting visitors to stare at an empty stretch of sand where a weary Spaniard once stood. Meanwhile, historians suspect his actual landing was near

Melbourne Beach, but unless the Melbourne Beach City Council decides to install an animatronic conquistador giving historically inaccurate monologues, it will likely remain in the shadow of St. Augustine's more theatrical claims.[n]

Ponce's return in 1521 did not end well. Intent on colonization, he landed this time on the Gulf side, possibly near Charlotte Harbor, only to encounter the Calusa, a Native American people who were unimpressed with his ambitions, and expressed their disapproval via projectile weaponry. One particularly well-aimed arrow, rumored to be poisoned, cut Ponce's plans short. He retreated to Cuba, where he promptly ceased being a problem for anyone.

And here we are, centuries later, with Ponce's name plastered across inlets, highways, and historical markers. The myth of the Fountain of Youth endures, because the notion that there exists a fix for mortality is simply too tantalizing to abandon (Dick Clark might have been able to enlighten us). And in St. Augustine, at least, the water still flows, offering visitors a sip of history—if not eternal youth, then at least a few moments of hopeful delusion. Which, in the end, might be close enough.

---

[n] I lived in Melbourne Beach for five years; there's a statue of Ponce on the beach there, holding his cross high and probably declaring "I discovered this place!" We experienced annual hurricanes so severe as to cause me to sell my waterfront "paradise" and move to France.

Chapter 67 King Arthur and the Sword in the Stone

The myth of King Arthur is one of the most famous legends in British folklore, blending history, mythology, and literary invention. Arthur is said to have been a great warrior and king who defended Britain against Saxon invaders in the late 5th or early 6th century. His story has evolved over centuries, incorporating elements of chivalry, magic, and divine kingship.

Mark Twain had Bing Crosby visiting the Knights of the Round Table in his book *A Connecticut Yankee in King Arthur's Court,* wherein a mechanic named Hank Martin uses plutonium and a flux capacitor to trick out a 1949 Jaguar XK120, so he could travel back in time and fall in love with Rhonda Fleming, who was magically babelicious.

One of the most famous aspects of the legend is the story of Excalibur, a magical sword that in some versions Arthur pulls from a stone, proving his divine right to rule. In other versions, Excalibur is given to him by a sorceress: because, as everyone knows, magical swords are generally distributed by mysterious women living in lakes.

Arthur's court at Camelot and his knights of the Round Table, including Sir Lancelot, Sir Gawain, and Sir Galahad, are said to have upheld the ideals of chivalry and embarked on quests, including the search for the Holy Grail, which they sought because their regular grails just weren't cutting it.

The question of whether Arthur was a real historical figure remains debated. There is no definitive contemporary evidence proving his existence, and early sources, such as the *Historia Brittonum* (written around the 9th century) and Geoffrey of Monmouth's *Historia Regum Britanniae* (12th century), mix history with legend. Some historians suggest that Arthur may have been based on a real leader, possibly a Roman-British warlord who fought the Saxons, but there is no archaeological proof of his reign or Camelot's existence.

Over time, the Arthurian legend has grown through medieval romances, especially in the works of writers like Chrétien de Troyes and Sir Thomas Malory. These stories introduced elements such as the love affair between Lancelot and Queen Guinevere, Merlin's magic, and the mystical Isle of Avalon.

So was Arthur real? We don't know. But his legend includes magic swords, time travel, questionable love triangles, and multiple musical numbers. Which, frankly, is more than most real kings ever gave us.

Chapter 68 Bigfoot/Sasquatch

Bigfoot, or *Sasquatch* (to give him the respect he deserves), lurks in the dark and misty forests of the Pacific Northwest like a ghost or a pooka that refuses to show itself, but loves the attention. The mere concept of the creature has contorted itself into a sort of running joke endlessly parroted by scores of "eyewitnesses" claiming to have glimpsed him.

Or "it." Whatever. The thing looks like a male of the species to me, in the pictures I've seen. For one thing, no boobs.

The reports are vague, unconvincing reflections of blurry outlines or snapshots of supposedly paranormal behavior, almost as elusive as the creature himself. But the intrigue is certainly there for that captivating, elusive...

...who or what was I talking about? Oh, yeah, "Bigfoot." Exciting stuff.

At least Sasquatch spotters were on the ball enough to snap some photos; why didn't Gladys Kravitz think to get her camera out to record Samantha Stevens' vexing antics? And why were *both* of the Darrins so dead-set against Samantha's sorcery? "Sam! No witchcraft," I can hear him whine. Essential questions of our time.

The drama of Bigfoot sightings, the half-glimpsed shadows and fuzzy photographs, creates a kind of hysteria at a low pitch. It is one of the longest treasure hunts in history (early settlers started reporting sightings in the late 1800s).

Perhaps the bounty is nothing but a strategically placed footstep in the mud. The search for Sasquatch has turned into a sport. Rather than the thrill of exciting and absurd hope, it comes with a set of quirky rules: No evidence is required, and lack of evidence may be good enough.

And consider the footprints: absurd yet entertaining artifacts of the Sasquatch narrative. They seem to be even bigger than the prints that "Harvey" might have left in the snow, had he followed James Stewart after his flaky angel "Clarence" from a different film changed Bedford Falls history. They're not just Bigfoot traces in the dirt; they are the soft, squelching punctuation marks of a story that can never quite end. Are the footprints real? They may have been the result of a wild bear who can play ape pretending to be 8-foot-tall ape. Perhaps. In the world of Mr. Sasquatch, the *mystery* is bigger than the *solution*, and every footprint and fuzzy photo represents breadcrumbs to nowhere.[o]

Like any good conspiracist knows, Bigfoot leaving such ambiguous clues only proves his intelligence, or at least his sarcasm. Giant footprints are a great way to spark imagination and get around detection. Here, the elusive Sasquatch is more than hiding; he is laughing too.

And maybe what is most remarkable about Bigfoot is how people approach the search. It is not the obsession over Sasquatch that is searching for truth, it is the search itself: that wonderful paradox where the less evidence, the better the story. It's as if the more unlikely Bigfoot is, the more people believe in him. It's a folk tale told with a dash of fun and absurdity, like a barroom fight over UFOs or about the Holy Grail. The lack of proof, or its deliberate evasion, seems to keep Bigfoot in the public mind. Or at least in the mind of Sasquatchians. Why are these wild tales so hypnotic? Maybe it's the elusive thought that something really magnificent is just out of sight, at the periphery of our comprehension. Maybe it's just the fun of the absurdity itself—that a creature this large could be so shy and elusive. Bigfoot may not care to reveal himself, but clearly, he knows how to keep us looking—and, for some, that is enough.

But for those who dare to value evidence? Well, Neil DeGrasse Tyson commented "You'd think that if an oversized ape-like mammal

---

[o] "Breadcrumbs to Nowhere" would be a good theme for a song.

were running around the forest, we'd have better data than a fuzzy video from the 1960s." [30]

In the end, the absence of Sasquatch is what makes him so compelling. The pursuit of a creature that may or may not exist is as rich with meaning as any treasure hunt, one that encourages us to imagine the unimaginable. And maybe the big guy knows the real joy isn't in being found, but in being endlessly speculated about. Like any good celebrity, he thrives in the realm of *what-if*, leaving behind a trail of footprints that lead not to answers, but to endless questions. If Bigfoot does exist, perhaps he is content to be nothing more than the world's most legendary game of hide-and-seek—one that never ends, but always manages to leave us wondering, "What if?" Or more likely, "WTF."

And maybe comedian Mitch Hedberg is right: the reason we don't have clear pictures is simply that Bigfoot himself is "blurry."

Sasquatch (artist's conception, non-blurry version)

Chapter 69 The Mysterious Bermuda Triangle

Where Maps and Sanity Go to Die

The Bermuda Triangle has occupied a peculiar space in the public imagination: a swirling vortex of paranoia, pseudoscience, and the world's most unreliable navigation systems. For decades, the disappearances of ships and aircraft in this murky stretch of ocean have been attributed to everything from malevolent sea monsters to interdimensional portals to an unholy Bermuda-exclusive brand of bad luck. However, as it turns out, the real explanation might not involve UFOs or the lost city of Atlantis, but something even more terrifying: physics.

Scientists, those relentless ruiners of perfectly good ghost stories, have pointed to rogue waves—massive, unpredictable, and so powerful that they could turn a cargo ship into a submerged paperweight in a matter of seconds. These waves, sometimes over 100 feet tall, form when the chaotic interplay of ocean currents and wind creates a moment of spectacularly bad hydrodynamic synergy. The Bermuda Triangle, conveniently located at the meeting point of the Gulf Stream, deep trenches, and some of the world's most capricious weather, is the kind of place where these monstrous waves like to make their entrance: dramatically, destructively, and with precisely zero concern for your fondness for smooth sailing.

Yet, despite this compelling explanation, the legends persist; because let's be honest, people would much rather believe in extraterrestrial abductions than in a particularly aggressive oceanic phenomenon. After all, if given the choice between an alien mothership and "water sometimes stacks up in weird ways," humanity will, nine times out of ten, go with the option that involves flashing lights and ominous music.

Flight 19

If ever there was an aviation incident desperately in need of Occam's razor, it's *Flight 19*, a squadron of five U.S. Navy TBM

Avenger bombers that, on December 5, 1945, embarked on a training exercise and promptly flew straight into history's favorite maritime conspiracy theory. Over the decades, their disappearance has been blamed on the Bermuda Triangle, malevolent extraterrestrials, wormholes, time travel, and—because why not—Atlantis. However, the real culprit was far less cinematic and infinitely more tragic: a disoriented pilot who didn't trust his compass.

Lieutenant Charles Taylor, *Flight 19*'s commander, was an experienced aviator with an unfortunate tendency to get lost; a fact conveniently omitted in most paranormal retellings. Shortly after takeoff, Taylor became convinced that his compasses were faulty and that the squadron had somehow ended up over the Florida Keys rather than the Atlantic. This was objectively false. His trainees, who still had functioning compasses (and, at this point, probably a sinking feeling in their stomachs), tried to correct him. He ignored them. Instead of steering west—toward land and safety—Taylor insisted on flying northeast, straight into the abyss.

What followed was a slow, avoidable descent into catastrophe. As fuel dwindled, the planes had no choice but to ditch into the ocean, where the choppy Atlantic waves ensured that whatever remained of *Flight 19* would never be seen again (the film *Close Encounters of the Third Kind* being an exception). Then, to put a neat little bow on the disaster, a rescue aircraft sent to find them exploded in midair, an event less indicative of supernatural interference and more of the Navy's longstanding love affair with flammable aviation fuel.

But facts, of course, have never been as entertaining as mystery. To this day, Flight 19 is trotted out as proof that the Bermuda Triangle is some kind of cosmic snare for unsuspecting ships and aircraft, rather than what it actually is: an exceptionally large stretch of water where bad things occasionally happen, mostly due to human error and bad weather. While people love a good enigma, they remain deeply unimpressed by the physics of fuel exhaustion and a stubborn refusal to make a left turn.

— **Easy Viewing** —

"The Unsolved WWII Aviation Mystery You've Never Heard of: Flight 19 and the Bermuda Triangle" www.youtube.com/watch?v=lkWagtTsNr8

Chapter 70 The Wendigo

The Wendigo is not just a monster; it is a catastrophic lapse in judgment given flesh, a spectral audit from the universe's Department of Overconsumption and Regret. Rooted in the folklore of Algonquian-speaking indigenous peoples (and unrelated to the "Round Table" of the same name), the Wendigo serves as a metaphysical cease-and-desist order against those who mistake desperation for permission.

The lore is breathtakingly simple and existentially horrifying: when faced with starvation, should a person succumb to the nuclear option of fine dining—that is, eating another person—they don't just violate social contracts. They void their warranty on being human entirely. The Wendigo is not a punishment in the traditional sense; it is a malfunction of existence itself, a permanent glitch in the operating system of one's own body. It stretches you out like an overused rubber band, tightens your skin into a jerky-adjacent texture, and turns your appetite into an unsolvable equation where the solution is always "more". The more you eat, the hungrier you become, a feedback loop of doom so perfectly designed that one suspects the universe has a dark sense of humor.

This is why the Wendigo is more than just another entry in the Cryptid-of-the-Month Club. It is a cosmic-level metaphor, a four-alarm existential crisis wrapped in a skeletal meat suit. Over the centuries, it has been retrofitted as a warning against everything from late-stage capitalism to environmental disaster, because if human civilization is good at anything, it is creating problems so large that they can only be described in terms of flesh-eating monsters. You know things have gone truly sideways when an ancient supernatural entity meant to deter cannibalism is also an accurate descriptor of Wall Street hedge funds.

And yet, at its core, the Wendigo isn't just about hunger. It's about the sheer audacity of taking too much. It is a walking, howling reminder that there is a fine line between survival and self-destruction, and that line is very, very thin when you're eyeing Dave from Accounting as a potential entrée. The final horror isn't that a Wendigo will find you in the woods—it's that, if given the right (or wrong) conditions, you might find one in the mirror.

No offense intended. But if you're feeling unusually hungry right now, maybe have a salad and think about your choices.

A wendigo (artist's conception)

Chapter 71 The Loch Ness Monster

Deep in the sullen, peaty gloom of Loch Ness, something lurks. Or doesn't. That's the beauty of it. The legend of Nessie is a masterclass in perplexity, the kind of riddle that thrives on its own deliberate ambiguity, much like a politician's stance on tax reform. One might think, given the ubiquity of high-resolution cameras and our apparent ability to count the individual nose hairs of Martian rovers, that we'd have a crisp, verifiable image of Scotland's most famous non-human resident. And yet, Nessie remains as stubbornly elusive as an honest résumé on Capitol Hill.

The well-known hoax photo

The loch itself is a geological relic with a personality disorder: deep enough to hide a prehistoric survivor (over 700 feet depth), murky enough to conceal the fact that it probably doesn't exist. Its waters are so impenetrably dark that if you submerged a high-powered spotlight, it would return its resignation letter in protest. Naturally, this opacity provides a convenient stage for our species' impressive ability to conjure monsters from the void, a skill we have honed from the caves of Lascaux to the Twitter replies of flat-earthers.

And yet, we persist. Nessie's most dedicated apostles exhibit a fascinatingly selective skepticism: they insist that the climate models of NASA and the National Academy of Sciences are "too uncertain" to warrant action, yet will point to a single, wobbly snapshot from 1934 as irrefutable evidence of a living plesiosaur. This is the same logic that allows people to believe in Bigfoot while simultaneously demanding to see Barack Obama's birth certificate.

Even more impressive is the creature's apparent MBA-level grasp of tourism economics. The frequency of reported sightings aligns with Scotland's high season so precisely that one suspects Nessie has a travel agent. She emerges at just the right intervals to keep the souvenir shops stocked with plush reptiles and vaguely amphibious shot glasses, but never so clearly as to risk becoming just another unfortunate *National Geographic* documentary. Like an aging rock band that keeps touring without releasing new material, Nessie knows the value of never quite confirming nor denying her presence.

Science, meanwhile, approaches Loch Ness with the same level of enthusiasm generally reserved for mandatory workplace training videos. The collective sentiment of the scientific community appears to be: "Look, if you people are still clinging to this, we have nothing but pity for you." However, local businesses are significantly less skeptical, because unlike marine reptiles, money is demonstrably real. Nessie has spawned a booming cryptozoological industry that seamlessly fuses folklore with capitalism, ensuring that every ripple in the water is either an ancient beast or, at the very least, a profitable ambiguity.

And so, the legend endures: a prehistoric paradox wrapped in myth and garnished with just enough perplexity to keep the cash registers ringing. Scotland, in its wisdom, embraces her, as one does a benevolent ghost or a particularly lucrative hallucination. Skeptics shake their heads, believers clutch their blurry photos, and the shopkeepers of Inverness nod approvingly, quietly hoping the mystery remains unsolved forever.

Because if there's one thing humans love more than the truth, it's a really good question that never quite gets answered.

Chapter 72 Mothman vs. Goatman

When I was in high school, the other kids told me about the legendary "Goatman," who, as you might imagine, was half goat and half man. Apparently he lived in the dark backwoods area south of Freeway Airport in Bowie, Maryland, possibly in the ditches off of that winding rural route known as Woodmore Road. I'm sure you've been there. I have, at night, and it was spooky.

Goatman is so famous, he's listed in the *Maryland Folklife Archives*.

But if you've never been to Point Pleasant, West Virginia, don't worry. Until 1966, neither had the Mothman, at least as far as anyone could prove.

Then, one fateful November night he arrived: a six-foot, glowing-eyed, flying menace whose main hobbies appeared to include terrifying teenagers and profoundly irritating the local authorities.

The first reported sighting came from two young couples, who were out driving near an abandoned munitions plant—because where better to conduct wholesome nighttime activities? According to them, a winged humanoid the size of a Buick suddenly emerged, with bright red eyes that gleamed with either supernatural menace or a solid commitment to winning a staring contest. Naturally, the couples did what any reasonable people would do: they floored it.

The Point Pleasant Register ran a story with a headline that, rather magnificently, failed to commit: "Couples See Man-Sized Bird… Creature… Something." (One assumes the editor resisted adding "…Or Maybe Just a Very Upset Egret?") Slow news day, no doubt.

Things escalated. More people saw the creature. A local dog went missing (surely you read about that). Theories ranged from "escaped government experiment" to "angry sandhill crane," the latter being a remarkably optimistic assessment of a situation involving glowing eyes and what several witnesses described as a profoundly unsettling presence.

Local law enforcement, caught between the rock of public hysteria and the hard place of not wanting to be the sheriff who arrested a giant bird monster, took the time-honored approach of waiting to see if the problem would just go away.

It did not. Reports continued. Conspiracy theories bloomed. The Mothman became a folk legend, a tourist attraction, and, naturally, an excuse for people to sell T-shirts.

And so, decades later, the legend persists. Whether the Mothman was an omen of doom, a cryptid with a flair for the dramatic, or just an overgrown owl with excellent PR, one thing is certain: if you ever find yourself in Point Pleasant, and you see a pair of glowing red eyes in the dark, maybe just keep driving.

And, *dear West Virginia*: I'll bet our Goatman could beat up your Mothman.

Part 5—Business Blunders

It's amazing how quickly things can go from brilliant to blundering, isn't it? One minute, an idea is hailed as the next big thing, the "game changer" that's going to reshape everything, and the next, it's a *Saturday Night Live* punchline. A shiny, expensive punchline. In the world of business, where egos are inflated with all the grace of a soufflé, it's not just about vision; it's about vision *plus* the ability to, you know, *see* what people actually need. You'd think that would be a prerequisite; but no, here we are, decades later, shaking our heads at the glorious train wrecks that were launched with enthusiasm but wrecked under the weight of bad planning and worse execution.

You might know the phrase *If it ain't broke, don't fix it*. Another one is *Don't spend time and money creating a product nobody needs*. And there's the simple *Know your shit*. But some people never learn these lessons.

Some of these blunders are laugh-out-loud funny: mistakes so large and so public, you could practically hear the facepalms echoing across the corporate boardrooms. A certain car manufacturer, convinced that its new model would revolutionize the market, instead revolutionized the concept of "unpopular." A certain tech company rolled out a product so ahead of its time that it was practically *too* ahead of its time—which is, of course, another way of saying it just didn't work. Then there were the disastrous re-brandings, the product lines that no one asked for, and the competition that couldn't see what was right in front of them until it was too late.

These stories are at once laughable, tragic, and in some cases, a little bit of both. But they also serve as a reminder: sometimes it's not about being the first to get to the finish line. Sometimes, it's about not tripping over your own feet on the way there. Or, if you must, doing it with a little more style, and a lot less expensive failure.

Chapter 73 Edsel

In the year 1958, Ford created the Edsel as a brand to alter the automotive industry's way of thinking. This, the company said, was more than just a car; it was a revolution; a leap forward into a bright new future of high-tech innovation and sleek modern design. Bold, visionary promises like this tend to get people all fired up, even though no one knows what the future itself is going to look like. Of course, the real trouble was that Ford appeared to have no better idea than a blindfolded chimpanzee playing darts as to what the public really wanted in a car.

The marketing campaign, which was monstrous and harried in equal measure, was designed by the Ford Motor Company to create interest for Edsel: a car that would be the car of a generation. Unfortunately, by the time Edsel was rolled out of the assembly line, he hardly resembled a car of the tomorrow. Instead, it appeared to be a concept car that had taken a wrong turn and ended up in production. Its front grille—something that can only be described as an attempt to make a car look like a malfunctioning insect—was instantly recognizable, but not in a good way. The dashboard appeared to be captured for a spaceship designed with so many buttons and switches that one would expect the car to orbit rather than just drive to the Winn-Dixie.

But aesthetics and design flaws aside, the real issue was that Ford simply misunderstood the market. Consumers in the late 1950s weren't begging for a futuristic, high-tech vehicle with more gadgets than a Bond villain's lair. Nor did they want a car that looked like it was designed by a first-year art student who'd just discovered cubism after one too many espressos and not enough vodka martinis.

Families wanted something practical, reliable, and easy to use; qualities the Edsel didn't exactly embody. And seventeen-year-olds, hopped up on the hotrod craze, wanted style and speed.

Speed, it had: a whopping 410 cubic-inch V-8 that produced 280 horsepower, able to scream at 114 miles per hour, given enough highway space. But no sane individual can picture Steve McQueen or Elvis driving one. Heck, even Howdy Doody would not be caught dead behind the wheel of one of these "futuristic" high-tech metal gargoyles.

Alfred E. Neuman, maybe.

The car's appeal was so narrowly defined, its features so over-engineered, that it alienated even the most enthusiastic potential buyers. The result was a monumental failure that went beyond a mere poor sales performance. The Edsel became synonymous with disaster (and anachronistically, "New Coke"), so much so that "Edsel" is still the go-to reference for any colossal misstep. The name itself became a punchline, a symbol of how even the most well-funded, well-marketed innovations can utterly collapse when they fail to understand their audience, their market.[31]

I won't go into the many problems with Tesla's Cybertruck except to say that Eric Noble, President of CARLAB and Professor at ArtCenter College of Design compared it unfavorably, saying: "It's right up there with Edsel. It's a huge swing and a huge miss."[32]

The Edsel wasn't just a car that didn't sell, it was a shining example of how blind ambition, combined with a complete lack of market insight, can turn even the most promising idea into a historic flop. Like the Tucker.

Or, the...

Chapter 74 Corvair

The Chevrolet Corvair, unleashed upon the American public in 1960, was Detroit's answer to a question nobody had really asked: "What if we put the engine in the back and just sort of...see what happens?" In a country where cars were traditionally built like rolling fortresses of chrome and excess, the Corvair was a rebellious little outlier: compact, air-cooled, and, according to some, hell-bent on delivering its occupants directly into the loving arms of the nearest emergency room.

Enter Ralph Nader, a man whose superpower was making even the most mundane aspects of consumer safety sound like a national emergency. His 1965 book *Unsafe at Any Speed* singled out the Corvair as a malevolent deathtrap, accusing it of possessing handling characteristics that could transform a Sunday drive into an impromptu physics experiment involving centrifugal force and sheer terror. To be fair, the first-generation models (1960-1963) did exhibit some, let's say, *eccentric* behavior. Thanks to a swing-axle suspension that demanded more finesse than the average American driver was accustomed to, the Corvair had a tendency to oversteer, meaning that if you weren't careful, you could find yourself facing the wrong direction, possibly while airborne.

But was the Corvair truly the homicidal maniac of the highway that Nader made it out to be? Not exactly. The real answer, much like the Corvair's handling, requires a bit of nuance. Yes, early models had quirks that could make life exciting in the same way that defusing a bomb with a rubber mallet might. But Chevrolet, realizing that customers generally preferred cars that didn't actively try to kill them, made significant improvements by 1964. They tweaked the suspension, added a stabilizer bar, and suddenly the Corvair was no more dangerous than any other car of the era; though, granted, that's a bit like saying a particular brand of cigarette is "no deadlier than the industry standard."

Unfortunately, the Corvair's reputation had already been dragged into the metaphorical guardrail. Nader's campaign painted it as the vehicular embodiment of corporate negligence, and in the ensuing public outcry, facts became secondary to fear. By 1969, Chevrolet—either exhausted from the bad press or just tired of explaining physics to the American public—pulled the plug on the Corvair. It was replaced by vehicles that were *technically* safer but also exponentially more boring.[33]

And yet, time has been oddly kind to the Corvair. Decades after its demise, it enjoys a cult following among those who appreciate its unconventional engineering and mid-century charm. It remains an automotive paradox: a car simultaneously condemned and cherished, an example of both innovation and the perils of pushing boundaries just a little too recklessly. Boxy, yes, and nothing Carroll Shelby would like to have been seen in, but it was also not the ogre that was the Edsel.

So, what can we learn from the Corvair's tumultuous history? First, that public perception often outweighs engineering reality. Second, that if you're going to introduce a radical new design, maybe don't cut corners on the suspension. And third, perhaps most importantly, that nothing guarantees a car's immortality quite like the claim that it was trying to kill people, regardless of who made such claims.

— Further Reading —

Fiore, Tony, *The Corvair Decade: An Illustrated History of the Rear Engined Automobile.* Corvair Society of America, 1980.

Chapter 75 Preston Tucker

The Tucker automobile, or as its friends called it, the Tucker 48, was the car that, like a soufflé, seemed to rise magnificently only to collapse under the weight of both its own ambition and an automotive conspiracy of epic proportions. Preston Tucker wasn't just making a car; he was making a statement: a glorious, chrome-and-steel fist aimed squarely at the chest of the automotive giants who were at the time wallowing in the comfort of postwar success. And let's face it, no one likes a show-off.

This car was like the prototype for the vehicles we should have been driving. The Cyclops Headlight? Who wouldn't want a headlight that turned with the steering wheel? (It's only decades later that modern cars have finally caught up, but don't mind that.) Then there was the rear-mounted engine, a radical departure from the front-engine norm that, in theory, improved safety and cabin space. (Did designers of the Corvair get their ideas from a failed automobile model?) In reality, it was like Tucker was asking the world to leap into the future with him, but the world wasn't quite ready for that kind of radical optimism. And let's be honest, when it came to innovative ideas, America's answer back then was usually "how about a more chrome bumper and fins like a jet plane?"

Tucker's safety features were so ahead of their time that they could have been snatched from an alternate universe. Reinforced steel safety cages, a padded dashboard, and a design that seemed to whisper, "Sure, let's make sure you don't die in a collision." Which, again, seemed a bit much to people who were still sorting out whether seatbelts were an unnecessary inconvenience. But it wasn't just the car that ruffled feathers; it was the whole damn idea of an outsider daring to take on the Big Three. GM and Ford were all too happy to pounce on Tucker, using their immense influence to discredit him. Tucker found himself drowning in legal charges—

specifically, securities fraud—a charge that was as nebulous as it was ultimately unproven. Nevertheless, the damage was done. Tucker was now public enemy number one, a figure who had to be crushed. By the time the dust settled, his dream had been rendered into 51 car-shaped relics, each one more a testament to corporate paranoia than to automotive innovation.

The Tucker 48's demise was both tragic and predictable. It was a beautiful idea strangled by the suffocating bureaucracy of both industry and government, a victim of its own brilliance. But like all great things, the Tucker 48 has achieved a kind of perverse immortality. Today, these 51 rare cars are collector's items worth millions, and Tucker himself, though crushed by the industrial machine, is now viewed as a tragic hero: a man whose vision was simply too large for the world he tried to change.

And so, the next time you see a Tucker 48, if ever, remember: it's not just a car. It's a reminder that the future, when it's too shiny and too new, is often the first thing the past will try to kill. Also only make an offer to buy it if you're serious.

— Further Reading —

Pearson, Charles T., *Indomitable Tin Goose: A Biography of Preston Tucker*. Pocket, 1988.

Lehto, Steve, *Preston Tucker and His Battle to Build the Car of Tomorrow*. Chicago Review Press, 2018.

Chapter 76 Sony Betamax

In the year 1975, the Japanese electronics company Sony launched the all-new Betamax technology, which was a revolutionary videotape format that seemed to belong to a future in which everything would inevitably be better: better picture, better quality sound, better fidelity. In many ways, it was an engineer's dream: sleek, polished, and undeniably superior. But, just as it happened many times in history, the superior product failed in a quite shocking manner and certainly not for lack of trying. Sony, with all its technical expertise, neglected the more mundane realities of business, like *selling* the thing.

For Sony, it was as if the quality of the product would do all the work. They created a machine that was a veritable marvel of modern technology, but it was also more expensive, more complicated to use, and required a series of niche components that made it less appealing to the average consumer. Betamax was, in many ways, the Ferrari of home video: impressive to those who could afford it or were technical enough to appreciate it. But the vast majority of consumers were just looking for a reliable way to watch movies without having to rewire their entire living room.

There was a brief copyright infringement battle, settled by the Supreme Court over the question of whether it was even legal to make copies of TV broadcasts.[34] In a 5-4 decision, they allowed us to tape stuff at home.

Meanwhile, the VHS format, which had all the elegance of a low-rent diner menu, was busy gaining traction by offering what Sony had overlooked: practicality. It didn't have the image quality Betamax had, but it worked. And it was *cheap*. In fact, VHS became the fast food of home video: widely available, easy to use, and with the backing of virtually every electronics manufacturer under the sun. While Sony was busy trying to create the ultimate cinematic experience, VHS was busy winning over everyone else by simply being... useful. VHS tapes also allowed two hours of recording time versus just one hour for Betamax.

By the end of the decade, Betamax, despite its superior picture quality, was outpaced and outclassed by VHS in a way that would become a textbook example of how a technically perfect product can fail if you miss the point. Betamax's greatest flaw wasn't its desire for viewing quality—it was that Sony had failed to consider the simplest fact of all: it's not about who has the better product, it's about who can make it *work* for everyone else. And in that, VHS was the overwhelming victor.

— Easy Viewing —

Engineerguy, "How Sony's Betamax lost to JVC's VHS Cassette Recorder." www.youtube.com/watch?v=ddYZlTaxlTQ

Chapter 77 Not MS-DOS

Gary Kildall: A name few of us knew, aside from those who have stumbled into a geeky documentary or gotten stuck at a nerdy dinner party. The guy who invented an operating system that would change everything was Kildall. CP/M was a clean, functional operating system for early computers—the stuff programmers depend on for as much as they depend on caffeine and the quiet of a server room. And the man should've been a god in Silicon Valley instead of the pathetic dude who got passed over like last year's smartphone model.

So, what happened? Well, in 1980 IBM, still possessed of grandiose technological visions, built a personal computer that changed everything. The only problem? The IBM made squat, expensive machines, but regarding software... well, their team probably needed a refresher course in 'How to make a Basic Operating System'. So naturally they said, "Go ask Gary Kildall." He's the guy. We'll make this work."

But Kildall didn't roll out the welcome mat, perhaps because he was infinitely wise, or perhaps because he was deeply involved in some engineering project involving a slide rule and a napkin. Word around the water cooler is that he wasn't available when IBM came knocking on his door. Maybe he was in a meeting, or maybe he chose arrogance and decided he could pick and choose when he wanted to become famous. But whatever the reason, Kildall missed the boat, and IBM, rather than pause and wonder, "What did we do?" kept moving forward.

Enter Bill Gates, who lacked the technical chops and the sexy appeal of a technology genius but knew how to make a deal. Gates needed no new operating system. He required a contract, and IBM was happy to accept. He got MS-DOS for free from Tim Paterson, who wrote some rudimentary stuff that looked like an old cash register, gave it a little polish, and called it a day. And there it was: Microsoft got its golden ticket. MS-DOS, a really limited, crappy OS.

What happened next is history. IBM got an operating system, Bill Gates became richest man in the world, and Gary Kildall, well, he was a tragic story of missed chances and tragic timing—like that guy at every tech conference that could have invented the next great thing but was thinking about something else. Kildall had that genius, that software, the vision. But he lacked the timing—and the hustle.

Kildall reminds us of something in tech that we tend to lose sight of: people. Often it isn't about who has the best ideas. It sometimes boils down to who knows how to make a deal and when to seize those fleeting chances the universe gives us. And maybe, just maybe, had Kildall picked up the phone, all of us would have KildallOS now. So here we are instead—scrolling around Windows and hearing people reminisce about what might have been.

In the end, the guy that comes along at the right moment and takes the deal wins, not always the very best idea. Not always. The universe rewards the bad guys. Or maybe it just awards it to the most opportunistic of people.

— Further Reading —

Evans, Harold, *They Made America: From the Steam Engine to the Search Engine*. 2004. [Contains a chapter on Gary Kildall, calling him the "forgotten father of the personal computer."]

Chapter 78 Ford Pinto

In 1970, Ford introduced the Pinto, a car that was supposed to be the crown jewel of affordable, compact American engineering. It was no Ferrari, but it was no Edsel either. With a design that was functional, if unremarkable, the Pinto promised the kind of fuel efficiency that would endear it to the masses. What could possibly go wrong? Well, as it turned out, everything. The Pinto had a singular, and rather explosive, flaw: its gas tank was positioned so poorly that in the event of a rear-end collision, it could, *and often did*, catch fire. Boom, you're in a car crash, and suddenly you're in the middle of an inferno. Not exactly what one might call "best-case scenario."

Now, you'd think a responsible company would have taken one look at that design flaw and said, "Well, this seems like a problem," and then fixed it. But Ford, the epitome of American corporate efficiency, decided to do something more Ford-like: they chose to ignore it. This wasn't a case of oversight. Ford knew about the flaw. Internal memos, studies, and grim reports all made it clear: the Pinto was a rolling death trap. And yet, Ford calculated that fixing the gas tank (a mere $11 per car) wasn't worth it. Why bother? The car was selling fine, and if a few people died, well, that's just part of the cost of doing business, right?

But as you know, shortcuts like this lead to the truth eventually. Accidents started piling up and people realized their Pintos were not only unreliable, they were deadly. Lawsuits were filed, the media jumped in like a bulldozer and Ford's once-solid reputation blew away. The Pinto could have been a forgettable car, but a case of corporate negligence demonstrated how cost-cutting can go from "lightly questionable" to "why did you think that was a good idea?"

In the end, Ford's great gamble, saving a few bucks to boost profits, cost them far more. They faced more lawsuits than they knew what to do with, a tarnished reputation, and the undeniable fact that sometimes, even in business, you simply can't put a price on human life. And that's the long and short of how the Pinto went from a compact car to a fiery cautionary tale.

— **Easy Viewing** —

1971 Chevrolet Impala Vs. 1972 Ford Pinto Full-Rear Impact (duration: 1:44). www.youtube.com/watch?v=lgOxWPGsJNY

Chapter 79 New Coke

After nearly a century of perfecting sugary refreshment, in 1985 Coca-Cola went fancy and reformulated its soda. They developed New Coke: sweeter, flashier and aimed at younger consumers. You know, those who could not stand a beverage that had long been a staple at every barbecue, every roadside gas station and every shady middle school vending machine. Evidently, Coca-Cola thought people wanted a sugar bomb and not, well, *Coke*. The company had decided that people didn't really want what they *wanted*; they wanted what Coca-Cola thought they should want.

And that, my friends, is how New Coke was born—a soda that was so sweet, you'd think they were trying to power the entire state of Texas on a sugar rush. The company, in its infinite wisdom, ignored the one thing that could never be calculated in any marketing meeting: *people have feelings about Coke*. They don't just *drink* it. No, they *love* it. Coca-Cola was America's sweet, brown elixir; it had become an institution, a cultural touchstone. So when the company announced it was going to change the formula, loyal customers were not pleased. At all.

What followed was not so much a backlash as a *revolution*. People wrote angry letters, called radio stations, and made so many complaints that Coca-Cola's customer service department probably started keeping tranquilizers in the office. In a shocking twist of corporate wisdom, Coke decided to ignore all of this for just long enough to watch the disaster unfold. The response was swift and brutal. Within months, Coca-Cola had to come crawling back, introducing *Coca-Cola Classic*, a backpedal so fast it nearly gave the company whiplash.

New Coke didn't just fail, it became a marketing joke of historic proportions. It went from being the "new" thing to the "most catastrophic decision in modern business history," quickly morphing into the sort of brand failure that marketing professors use as a warning to never, *ever* mess with a formula that has been working for decades. It's the kind of thing you can't forget. To this day, *New Coke* is mentioned in the same breath as other corporate mistakes like the Edsel. Hell, even *The Simpsons*—that acid-tongued oracle of popular culture—had a moment in which New Coke got skewered, with Danny DeVito's voice perfectly encapsulating the whole *what-were-you-thinking?* vibe.

Coca-Cola learned the hard way that sometimes, changing things that aren't broken doesn't just fail, it explodes in your face like a can of soda in the car backseat of a Florida summer. The product wasn't just a failure. It was an entire marketing campaign's worth of mistakes wrapped up in one overly sugary bottle of effervescent, dark brown regret.

— **Further Reading** —
Pendergrast, Mark, *For God, Country, and Coca-Cola*. Basic Books, 2013.

— **Easy Viewing** —
The Simpsons - New Coke (duration: 8 seconds)
www.youtube.com/watch?v=uXg1ge27vgo

Chapter 80 Apple's Newton

Blinded by their own vision of the future and perhaps a little too much fuel from Silicon Valley ambition, in 1993 Apple unleashed the Newton: a cross between a clipboard and an Etch a Sketch. It was a "Personal Digital Assistant," or PDA in the new parlance of the times, and it bore all the trademarks of a world-changing device: a compact, portable computer that held your notes, your contacts, and your schedule. Think of it as the '90s jetpack. Well, sort of.

The future was supposed to be at hand. The present universe was supposed to have a cutting-edge technology that would recognize the handwriting, yet it ended up being another product people look back on and laugh at. It was like a calculator that couldn't add, a toaster that couldn't toast, or a Cuisinart that couldn't… cuisine. Apple, in their eagerness to change the world, had released a product that couldn't do the very thing it was supposed to: recognize handwriting.

But it wasn't just the bugs that sank the Newton—it was the timing. The Newton came out at a moment when the world wasn't quite ready to carry a computer in their pocket, let alone one that was as clunky as an old VCR. It was expensive, unrefined, and lacked the magic touch that made gadgets truly irresistible. People wanted their phones to, well, *make calls.* They weren't yet ready to put a tiny computer in their pocket that would, at best, mess up their to-do lists and send autocorrect-style letters to their bosses.

The Newton's short-lived existence became one of those tech disasters you look back on and laugh at. And not just tech geeks: once again *The Simpsons* weighed in. One of the bullies, "Dolph," writes in cursive on his Newton, "*Beat up Martin.*" The Newton interprets it as "Eat up Martha." If a cartoon is mocking your product, you know it's over.

The Newton, in the end, did not just crash and burn; it glided across concrete for a while, hit a few curbs, and then blew up to an extent that sent shock waves through Apple's reputation.

However, here is the rub: This wasn't simply a failed product; while tripping over its own feet, it predicted the future. Years down the line, smartphones would be the true embodiment of the dream of the Newton that was tried but failed. The world just wasn't ready for its shiny, eccentric, overpriced cousin back in the '90s. The price tag was about $800, or $1,800 in today's dollars.

Thus, the Newton took its rightful place among a pantheon of incredibly odd fads; the pet rock, DeLorean, and mullets: a chuckle at best. Yet, an embarrassing relic of an era wherein the future tried to elbow its way into existence way too early.

— Further Reading —

Honan, Mat, *Wired*. "Remembering the Apple Newton's Prophetic Failure and Lasting Impact." Aug 5, 2013.
wired.com/2013/08/remembering-the-apple-newtons-prophetic-failure-and-lasting-ideals/

Chapter 81 Kodak's Digital Camera Hesitation

At one time, Kodak signaled photography. Really, it was almost the name in capturing the human experience. Kodak, reigning royal over nostalgia, ruled the empire of film: a vast kingdom of yellow boxes occupied by a single bored clerk and filled with photochemical magic. Every family trip, every birthday party, every embarrassing teenage crush was preserved on Kodak film. But here's the kicker: Kodak did not simply dominate film; it had the digital camera tucked away in its inner pocket, waiting for the world to catch up.

In 1975, Kodak engineer Steven Sasson developed the first digital camera. So yeah, wise-old Kodak had the digital camera before anyone else even thought about making the switch away from film. But instead of pushing into the digital wonderland, Kodak did what every *half-a-dozen-billion-dollars-later* corporate body does best: it just sat there. Kodak saw this shiny new toy and said: "Hmmm, seems fun, but let's hold off on this whole 'digital' thing. We're making money off film, folks. Why fix what isn't immediately broken?"

And so Kodak, which could have been the Apple of Photography, played it safe. They stuck to film. *Film.* Remember those? The technological equivalent of a steam engine, while the rest of the world was rolling out electric and gas-powered cars. Meanwhile, digital camera production was zooming ahead and capturing market share quicker than you can say, "exposure triangle," by competition such as Canon and Sony.

The result? Kodak, which had invented the very thing that would later *define* photography in the 21st century, spent the next few decades being the equivalent of the guy who still insists on using a rotary phone when everyone else has an iPhone. It wasn't pretty. As digital photography became the norm, Kodak's insistence on sticking to its film-based business model looked less like "forward-thinking innovation" and more like "dustin' crops where there ain't no crops."

By the time Kodak finally realized that digital photography wasn't just a fad, it was too late. The digital revolution had already swept through the photography industry, leaving Kodak gasping for air. It was as if Kodak had missed the memo that the world was changing. In 2012, after years of slow-motion corporate self-destruction, Kodak filed for Chapter 11 bankruptcy protection. A company that once stood at the pinnacle of tech innovation had become a cautionary tale about the dangers of clinging to the past. It was like watching a giant dinosaur holding on to its favorite tree, completely unaware that a meteor was heading straight for it.

But its tale is wonderfully tragic because Kodak did not invent the future, it avoided it. This is the technological equivalent of inventing the computer and then saying, "No, we're going to stick with the slide rule for a few more decades." And if Kodak's downfall was sadly instructive, it was also an indication that finding the new important thing is only part of innovation; it takes guts to realize when to part with the old useless one.[35]

Chapter 82 Blockbuster vs. Netflix

Once upon a time, Blockbuster Video was the king of all things rental. Its stores were everywhere: big, bold, and brash with their blue-and-yellow signs and towering shelves of VHS tapes that promised you a weekend of cinematic bliss. You didn't just rent movies at Blockbuster; you *experienced* them. You could spend an hour wandering the aisles, picking up a random tape from the sci-fi section just because it had a cool cover, only to hit "play" and realize you'd rented a 120-minute instructional video on septic tank maintenance. But hey, it was the '90s and things were simpler.

And then, one fateful day in the early 2000s, a small startup named Netflix knocked on Blockbuster's door, .offering to sell itself for the ridiculously low price of $50 million. If you're sitting there thinking, "How in the world did Blockbuster turn that down?" Well, you're not alone. Netflix, at the time, was a DVD-by-mail service, a quirky little online outfit with a great idea but not much else. Blockbuster, of course, was the heavyweight of the video rental world, with hundreds of stores and millions of film enthusiasts and popcorn eaters. But here's the thing: Blockbuster didn't just say, "No, thanks." They essentially scoffed at the idea, dismissing Netflix as a niche, fleeting trend.

The problem with this, of course, is that the world was changing faster than Blockbuster's executives could say "late fee." While Blockbuster was still obsessed with its physical stores, Netflix had a very simple idea: "Hey, how about we just ship DVDs to your house and let you keep them as long as you want, without any late fees?" Blockbuster, apparently thinking that the consumer's love for waiting in line at a store was boundless, didn't see the writing on the wall. Or, more accurately, it was too busy trying to figure out how to charge people more for late rentals to care about anything so radical as an online subscription.

As the 2000s wore on, Netflix transitioned from DVDs in the mail to the future of entertainment: *streaming*. And while Netflix was busy creating a future where you could watch movies on your phone while sitting in your wine-stained PJs, Blockbuster was still hanging onto the dream of the in-store rental experience. The result? Blockbuster got steamrolled. Not only did Netflix steal the thunder, but it also ended up becoming *the* go-to platform for on-demand entertainment, forcing Blockbuster into a weird, futile game of catch-up. The inevitable bankruptcy followed in 2010, and Blockbuster's legacy became the punchline of a thousand "what not to do in business" speeches.

Blockbuster's downfall isn't just a business failure. It's a shining example of how a massive, once-invincible company can be flattened by its own inability to adapt. Netflix wasn't just the future, it was the future *everyone* was looking for, except Blockbuster. And by the time Blockbuster finally figured it out, Netflix was sitting on its mountain of cash, streaming every episode of *The Office* you could possibly want, while Blockbuster had storerooms of leftover VHS tapes nobody wanted to rent anymore. It's like the guy who insists on buying the world's last fax machine while everyone else is texting. It's over before you even realize it's begun.

— Further Reading —

Randolph, Marc, *That Will Never Work: The Birth of Netflix and the Amazing Life of an Idea*. Back Bay Books, 2019.

Chapter 83 Yahoo Missed Google

It's the kind of story that makes you want to slap your forehead in exasperation. In 1998, Google offered to sell its technology for a mere $1 million. Nobody bit the hook. A million dollars? Chump change. By 2002, Yahoo realized the potential for search engine technology, and offered a tad more than Google's original proposal: this time it was $3 billion. Google countered with $5 billion, and Yahoo walked away. Why would Yahoo bet on a glorified search engine when they could keep flogging their own tired online directory?

Google, you see, was doing something different. Something that would revolutionize how we interact with the web. But Yahoo, that once-unstoppable force of the early web, couldn't see past the curtain of its own success. They thought they knew the internet. They were convinced that they were in control. The truth was, they were too busy being the Kings Of The Old Way Of Doing Things to realize that a new king was emerging. A king who would not only dominate the search engine world, but also the very way we think about advertising.

In a sense, Yahoo wasn't wrong. At the time, no one could really have predicted that a search engine would grow into the behemoth that Google has become. But Yahoo had a front-row seat to history and still managed to look the other way. It's the same kind of thinking that keeps people from recognizing the next big thing. We're all too busy with our comfortable little ways to imagine that the world might change. Yahoo's arrogance—and its inability to acknowledge Google's potential—was its undoing.

Today, Google is worth about $2 trillion.[36]

Chapter 84 The Peugeot 1007

In 2004, Peugeot's engineers, probably with too much coffee (or wine) and an ungodly amount of overtime, decided to get clever. They thought, "Why not make a small car even smaller with a door that slides open... electronically!" Yeah. That's how the 1007 model was born. The problem? The door didn't want to slide. It didn't want to do anything other than break down. And, naturally, that's what it did. Constantly. It wasn't just the door. The whole car was like that friend who tries to impress everyone with something new, only to forget they've never done it before.

But Peugeot's mistakes weren't just technical. Oh, no. They made the critical error of forgetting one thing: buyers don't like expensive tech in a small car. The cost to buy and maintain this thing was absurd for what it offered. People wanted cheap, cheerful city cars. They didn't need an engineering masterpiece that would last approximately two days before the electric sliding door malfunctioned and you got stuck in the car like a hamster in a wheel.

The 1007 was a disappointment that never ends. It was expensive, had a gizmo-laden door that could have been designed by the ghosts of failed technology past and lacked the simplicity people wanted in daily drivers. It was trying to be everything without being anything. Why? Because it was too fancy for its own good. Too complex for a car that was supposed to be as easy as a cup of coffee on a Monday morning. Peugeot didn't make a car, they made a very expensive experiment. They seem to have been victims of an engineering blunder we call "feature creep."

But, hey: credit where it's due. Peugeot didn't just curl up in a ball and weep. No, after the 1007, the company realized they needed to be a bit more... grounded. So, they made a comeback. By 2008, models like the 308, 208, and 3008 weren't just functional, they were good. Really good. Efficient, sleek, and reliable cars for the masses. The

1007 was, in hindsight, a painful lesson, but it also taught Peugeot how to move forward. And forward they went, becoming a more prominent, globally recognized brand.

By the way, I moved from the US to France in 2021, and bought a Peugeot (5008 model). It's a nice car, just a little too big for some of the narrow, winding streets you encounter in the smaller towns, especially in the rustic old country villages.

But I digress, as I sometimes find myself doing. In the end, Peugeot found itself, much like the kid who tried to pull off the high-flying skateboard trick and got sent to the ER, dusted itself off, and figured out how to stick the landing. Now, as part of Stellantis, it has a global reach and a reputation for making solid, reliable cars that, *thankfully*, don't have electric sliding doors to break. The Peugeot 1007 may have been the car equivalent of a "what were they thinking?" moment, but Peugeot? They're still around, still innovating, and still reminding us that even the worst missteps can lead to something better.[37]

— **Further Reading** —
Fowler, George, et. al., *Car-tastrophes: 80 Automotive Atrocities from the past 20 years.* Veloce, 2020.

Chapter 85 Toyota Gas Pedal Recall

Imagine, if you will, the automotive equivalent of a horror movie. You're cruising along, minding your own business, when all of a sudden your car's accelerator pedal decides to play a little game of "No, I think I'll stay stuck right here, thank you very much." And, with that, the Toyota recall debacle of 2009 begins. Now, you may have heard of Toyota, that car company that had built an empire on making cars that didn't explode, didn't fall apart, and didn't leave you stranded by the side of the road. Unlike many American brands, the clocks in their dashboards even worked. Well, in the late 2000s, Toyota was riding high—so high, in fact, that they were pretty much the world's largest automaker. They were doing everything right. They were like the geeky kid who aced every test and brought the right lunch to school. But then—bam! They forgot to check the homework. And they couldn't claim the dog ate it.

In the autumn of 2009, Toyota was forced to recall over 8 million cars. And why? Toyota accelerator pedals had decided to turn into overzealous gymnasts, getting stuck in the full-throttle position when they weren't supposed to. This is not exactly a feature you want in a car, especially when you're in traffic or, heaven forbid, trying to parallel park. Suddenly, that reliable Toyota Corolla you had come to trust was behaving more like a runaway shopping cart on a hill. Not exactly what you want from a vehicle that had long been the symbol of solid, no-nonsense engineering.

Faulty linkage? Loose bolts? Well, "mechanical sticking" was part of the problem. Also, their floor mats had a tendency to slide under the gas pedal causing it to stick, so they changed the shape of the pedal.

It was a monumental screw-up, and like all monumental screw-ups, it made you wonder how it could have gone so wrong. Toyota, of course, immediately issued the recall, but by that point, the damage had already been done. This was no longer about fixing some faulty pedals; this was about fixing the global image of a company that was supposed to be above all that.

The public relations response, you'll be shocked to learn, was not exactly *swift* or *clear*. Toyota, who had once moved with the speed and grace of a sleek Japanese train, now seemed to be moving at the pace of an old man trying to find his glasses. They initially claimed the only problem was with the floor mats. And by the time they admitted that the pedals had problems, well, let's just say that trust in the company was officially in the "not good" zone.

And yet, the real comedy of this situation wasn't just that the world's largest automaker had let this happen. It was that Toyota, for all its mechanical wizardry, had no idea how to handle a PR disaster of this magnitude. They had a decades-long reputation for precision engineering, but fixing the PR mess? They seemed unable to realize that, when you're stuck in deep doggy doo-doo, you need to exit the mess and clean it up as soon as you can. Meanwhile, across the Pacific, the American automakers were rubbing their hands together in delight. Finally, someone else had messed up worse than Detroit had.

Of course, Toyota, despite all of this, survived and even thrived. They're still around, selling cars, making money, and giving you that comforting "Toyota-quality" feeling when you get behind the wheel. But for a while there, it wasn't just about fixing pedals; it was about a company trying to restore the faith of millions of drivers, who had just realized that maybe their trusty Corolla wasn't quite as trustworthy as they thought.

In the end, Toyota learned that even when you're making cars that can go for a million miles without a hiccup, you're never more than one sticky pedal away from turning your world upside down. And for a brief, glorious moment, it looked like the world's most beloved automaker had forgotten how to make a car that didn't want to kill you.[38]

Chapter 86 The Nokia Smartphone Decline

Once upon a time, in the mythical age before TikTok and battery anxiety, there was Nokia. And if you didn't own one of their phones, you were either very unlucky or a time traveler from the future who had somehow arrived at the turn of the millennium without one. Nokia phones were everywhere. They were reliable. They were indestructible. You could drop them, throw them, use them to fend off an aggressive seagull, and they would still work. You could probably use one to hammer in a nail and then call your mom on it to brag about your superior craftsmanship.

And then, one day, Nokia vanished. Not overnight, not in a dramatic, *poof*-of-smoke kind of way, but in that slow, painful manner reserved for once-great institutions that fail to notice they are becoming obsolete until they are *very* obsolete. One moment, Nokia was the unchallenged king of mobile phones. The next, it was like an aging rock band that refused to stop releasing new albums, blissfully unaware that the audience had moved on.

What happened? Well, in short: Apple. Then Google. Then the unstoppable march of technological progress, combined with Nokia's insistence that everything was *fine, actually*, right up until the point where it very clearly wasn't.

Nokia's great mistake—aside from failing to realize that time moves forward and people enjoy things that are better than the things they had before—was clinging to Symbian, an operating system that felt like it had been designed by a committee of time travelers from 1998 who had never actually seen a modern touchscreen. It was clunky. It was slow. It was the technological equivalent of trying to run a Formula 1 race with a horse and buggy.

Meanwhile, Apple had introduced the iPhone; a device so futuristic that it made everything else look like an artifact from a lost civilization. Google followed suit, unleashing Android into the world, and suddenly, the entire phone industry had changed. Except Nokia. Nokia was still standing in the corner, quietly insisting that people loved Symbian, even as those very people were lining up outside Apple Stores to trade their Nokias for something, *anything else*.

By the time Nokia realized it was in trouble, it was *really* in trouble. The company eventually flailed its way into a desperate alliance with Microsoft, resulting in a series of Windows Phones that were technically competent but had all the mass appeal of a spreadsheet convention. People weren't interested. The few who were interested had to deal with an app store that contained roughly six apps, two of which were weather widgets.

And so, Nokia's fall ended not with a bang, but with an acquisition. Microsoft bought its phone business in 2014, presumably because it was feeling nostalgic for the 1990s and thought, "Hey, maybe we can make this work." Spoiler: they could not. Within a few years, Nokia's phone division had been dismantled, leaving behind nothing but the lingering echoes of old ringtones and the collective regret of thousands of executives who had once believed they were untouchable.

And so, Nokia became the corporate equivalent of a tragic folk song: once mighty, now gone. It wasn't lack of talent that killed it. It wasn't even competition. It was the quiet, creeping arrogance of believing that being on top means you will *stay* on top, as we have seen time and again within the pages of this book.

— **Further Reading** —
Doz, Yves L., *Insead*. "The Strategic Decisions That Caused Nokia's Failure."
knowledge.insead.edu/strategy/strategic-decisions-caused-nokias-failure

Chapter 87 Samsung Galaxy Note

More Explosive News

Let's talk about the Samsung Galaxy Note—specifically, the Note 7, or as it came to be known in certain circles: *That Phone That Might Explode but Only When You're Not Looking Directly at It.*

Now, the Galaxy Note series started off innocently enough. The first few models were basically what you'd get if a smartphone and a legal pad had an overachieving baby who also happened to be a personal assistant and part-time graphic designer. The Note was big. Really big. Holding one up to your face made you look like you were trying to FaceTime someone using a hardcover book. But it *worked*. It was flashy, functional, and just serious enough to make you feel like you were working even if you were mostly just Googling whether or not you could microwave aluminum foil.

Then came 2016. Enter: the Note 7.

The Note 7 was supposed to be the apex predator of smartphones. It had a stylus, iris scanning, curved glass, and, *get this*, a battery with a personality. Unfortunately, that personality was *angry*. And flammable.

In fairness to Samsung, the phone was beautiful. Sleek. Precise. It had that kind of techno-erotic allure usually reserved for sci-fi props and high-end espresso machines. But beauty, as it turns out, is only touchpad-deep. Go a few millimeters deeper, and you got what appeared to be a tiny lithium-based warhead with trust issues.

People started reporting that their brand-new Note 7s were doing things phones generally shouldn't do, such as self-heating to nuclear-adjacent levels, venting smoke, and in rare but memorable cases, going full Michael Bay. You know that old Energizer Bunny ad? Imagine it with the bunny suddenly exploding and taking out your car's cupholder.

Samsung, ever the corporate trapeze artist, quickly launched a recall. They swapped out the defective units for what they claimed were "safe" ones, which is sort of like swapping a bear trap for a slightly newer bear trap and telling everyone it's fine now because this one's *painted blue*.

It didn't work.

The replacement units began doing the same thing. At this point, airlines started treating the Note 7 like it was a tiny box of C-4 with a touch screen. There were announcements at every gate: *"If you are carrying a Samsung Galaxy Note 7, you may not board this flight unless you surrender it, and possibly yourself, to federal authorities."*

Eventually, after the public relations equivalent of a flaming zeppelin crash, Samsung gave up. On October 10, 2016, they pulled the plug. Permanently. The Note 7 was yanked from production, sales, and polite conversation. It joined the pantheon of great tech disasters, somewhere between Betamax and New Coke, though admittedly more likely to burn your pants off.

The aftershocks were financial and reputational. Samsung had to explain, over and over, that their devices were no longer mobile fire hazards. Engineers performed a post-mortem that read like a medical mystery script: casing too tight, welding defects, tab A inserted into slot *oh no*. Samsung eventually released a very, very thorough battery safety report, which had the faint air of an apology delivered by someone who once crashed your car but now owns a driving school.

The Galaxy Note line continued for a while, like a comeback tour from a band whose lead singer had spontaneously combusted on stage. And for a few years, it sort of worked.

But the Note 7? That model will forever be remembered as the smartphone that tried to be everything… and nearly *detonated* trying.

Chapter 88 Theranos

The Wellness Scam That Bled America Dry

Theranos was supposed to be the future. And it was, if your vision of the future includes delusion, unblinking confidence, and people in expensive suits nodding solemnly at gibberish. You remember Elizabeth Holmes, the wide-eyed founder with the voice of a Batman villain and the wardrobe of a *Black Mirror* extra. She promised a world in which a single drop of blood could tell you everything from your iron levels to whether or not you'd been cursed by a 13th-century gypsy witch.

Enter the "Edison" machine: a shoebox-sized altar of tech mysticism, allegedly capable of running hundreds of medical tests using barely enough blood to give a mosquito diabetes. It was the Holy Grail of diagnostics. Also, it was a toaster with a God complex. It didn't work—which, in Silicon Valley, is sometimes less a bug and more of a branding strategy.

Still, investors lined up like it was the sequel to Netflix, but with more bodily fluids. Walgreens bought in. Kissinger joined the board. Madeline Albright showed up. People who should have known better—and *did* know better, but were distracted by the word "disruption"—got suckered in like it was the Church of Scientology, but with pipettes.

Meanwhile, inside Theranos HQ, chaos reigned. If a test failed (which it did, often), the fallback plan was: run the blood on someone else's machine, put a sticky note over the brand, and declare victory. It was a little like opening a Michelin-starred restaurant that serves takeout from Arby's in hand-thrown ceramic bowls.

Holmes, meanwhile, delivered press interviews like a giddy HAL 9000 giving a TED Talk. Her voice, her turtlenecks, her eerie detachment from the physical world, all curated to scream "visionary," when in fact the only vision involved was the kind you get after snorting ergot-tainted flour. When she was interviewed early on, age 19, pointing out she was "the youngest billionaire in the world," she commented, "You know, it's not what matters. What matters is how well we do in trying to make people's lives better."³⁹ So selfless and altruistic!

Then, like a plot twist written by Kafka while blackout drunk on NyQuil, John Carreyrou from *The Wall Street Journal* did what venture capitalists and the FDA somehow could not: ask basic questions. He peeled back the latex gloves and revealed the operation for what it was: a kind of sterile Ponzi scheme for people with Fitbits and unearned optimism.

The consequences came fast, if not furious. Holmes was convicted on four counts of fraud in 2022 and sentenced to 11 years in prison. Sunny Balwani, her COO and human firewall, earned a matching sentence; possibly the first time in legal history that *his and hers* felony convictions were handed down like an anniversary gift. They were also ordered to pay about *half a billion* in restitution to the victims of the fraud.

And the Edison machine? Nowhere. Probably hiding in a Palo Alto storage unit between a Segway prototype and the original Ford Pinto, both of which, it should be noted, had the decency to explode *openly*.

The whole thing reads like a rejected *Black Mirror* episode: promising, creepy, and somehow too plausible to be funny. Except it *is* funny, if you've got a taste for schadenfreude and understand that the true diagnostic test for a broken system is whether someone can raise billions of dollars promising medicine that never worked, to people who never asked why.

Theranos didn't just fail. It exposed the modern fetish for "visionaries" who, when you scratch off the varnish, turn out to be carnival barkers with PowerPoint decks and Giorgio Armani garb. They called it a unicorn. They were right, in that it was mythical, dangerous, and you wouldn't want to ride one into surgery.

Somewhere, a burned-out investor is still muttering, "But she *seemed* so convincing." And somewhere else, the ghost of the Ford Pinto is whispering, "Amateur."

Chapter 89 The Volkswagen Emissions Scandal

Volkswagen, that beloved German automaker long associated with reliability, efficiency, and the ability to produce vehicles that somehow manage to be both boring and expensive, pulled off one of the most breathtaking acts of corporate deception in modern history. And not in a small, amateurish way, like fudging a few numbers on a balance sheet. No, they went all-in, creating an elaborate high-tech lie so brazen, so ingeniously sinister, that if it weren't actively poisoning the atmosphere, you'd almost have to admire the sheer effort.

Here's how it worked. Volkswagen's diesel cars came with a secret software program: a sort of digital *Jekyll-and-Theranos* routine. When the car sensed it was being tested for emissions, it politely pretended to be an environmental saint, purring along within the legal pollution limits like an obedient, regulation-abiding machine. But once the test was over and the car hit the road? It transformed into a rolling smog factory, belching out toxic emissions at levels that would make a 1950s steel mill blush.

This was not a small-scale con. This was a global, multi-year, billion-dollar, Bond-villain-level scam, with over 11 million affected vehicles polluting at up to 40 times the legal limit. The sheer commitment to dishonesty is almost endearing—this wasn't just one or two guys in a dark office with a laptop and a bad idea. No, this was an entire team of engineers, executives, and probably a few highly paid consultants sitting around a conference table, nodding in agreement as someone pitched, "What if we just... don't make the cars cleaner, but we *trick* everyone into thinking we did?"

When regulators finally caught on in 2015—after years of Volkswagen smugly touting their "clean diesel" technology like it was a gift from the gods—the backlash was seismic. Lawsuits. Criminal charges. Billions in fines. Executives resigning in droves. Suddenly, the company that had spent decades cultivating an image of precision and integrity found itself looking less like an automaker and more like the world's least competent crime syndicate.

The best (or worst) part? They absolutely didn't have to do this. Volkswagen could have just, you know, built cleaner engines. They had the money. They had the technology. But instead, they chose to invest in an elaborate, multi-layered act of fraud, which raises the question: at what point in the meeting did someone say, "Let's spend a fortune developing technology that tricks emissions tests instead of spending that same fortune on developing, say, *actual* emissions-reducing technology," and at what point did everyone else *agree*?

In the years since, Volkswagen has desperately tried to rebrand itself as a leader in electric vehicles, hoping that people will forget about that time they flooded the Earth with toxic gas while pretending to be the *Captain Planet* of car manufacturers. And sure, maybe they've turned over a new leaf. Maybe they're genuinely committed to sustainability now. But given their track record, one has to wonder: when you plug in a Volkswagen electric car, does it actually charge, or does it just *pretend* to?

So it seems that if a corporation loudly declares itself to be ethical, responsible, and environmentally conscious, assume, as a general rule, that they are up to something truly horrifying. And if they start calling themselves a leader in green technology, check under the hood. They might just be running a software update on the scam.

— **Further Reading** —
EPA, "Volkswagen Light Duty Diesel Vehicle Violations for Model Years 2009-2016." www.epa.gov/vw

Part 6 – War and/or Peace

You know the song: What is it good for? Sometimes good for a laugh, sometimes a learning experience, most often good for a cry. We are often told that it is "hell." But what we are not told nearly enough is that it is also frequently idiotic—a vast, gruesome theater of human ingenuity gone completely off the rails. While great minds have spent centuries devising new and improved ways to reduce cities to smoking craters, they have also, for reasons beyond rational comprehension, spent a good deal of time dreaming up some of the most asinine concepts ever to be taken seriously by people with actual ranks and budgets.

Consider, if you will, the bat bomb: a plan to strap tiny incendiary devices to living bats and release them over Japanese cities in the hope that they would roost in buildings and set everything ablaze. This was a real thing. Taxpayer dollars were involved. Then there was the pigeon-guided missile, which, because the war effort wasn't already teetering on the brink of lunacy, involved strapping live pigeons into missile guidance systems and letting them peck their way toward victory. Military science, ladies and gentlemen.

And then there's the Giant Panjandrum, which sounds like something out of Lewis Carroll but was, in fact, an actual careening, flaming, rocket-propelled wheel of destruction that worked about as well as you'd expect. That is to say, it did not work at all. Meanwhile, the Maginot Line—France's extraordinarily expensive attempt at saying, "I fart in your general direction"—stood as a monument to brilliantly engineered irrelevance, blocking an invasion route that no one was planning to use while leaving the actual invasion route wide open. A+ for effort. F for results.

And yet, war also has its brief, accidental interludes of sanity. In 1914, British and German soldiers took a break from the grand, industrial-scale carnage of World War I to play a Christmas football match in No Man's Land. The next morning, they resumed killing each other, because war is nothing if not consistently stupid.

But perhaps the greatest wartime wonder of all is the Monopoly escape kits: ordinary board games, distributed to British POWs, that had been secretly modified to include maps, compasses, and actual money to aid in escape attempts. Yes, Monopoly, the game that normally reduces entire families to screaming dysfunction, was once used as a highly effective tool for getting out of a German prison camp.

War is, if nothing else, a showcase of human extremes. It is destruction and horror, but it is also farce, delusion, and occasional moments of strange, accidental genius. In this section, you will find all of these things, neatly packaged and historically verified, so that you may fully appreciate the fact that while war may be a disaster, it is, on occasion, an absolutely fascinating one.

Chapter 90 Andersonville

Andersonville Prison, officially known as Camp Sumter, was less a prison than a sustained exercise in human suffering: so profound that even Stephen King might have struggled to conjure a horror story more hideous.

Established in 1864 by the Confederacy to house Union prisoners of war, it quickly devolved into an ungovernable hellscape where 33,000 men were crammed into a space meant for a third of that number. Water was scarce, disease was rampant, and the guards—whether through malice or sheer indifference—watched as their captives withered under a pitiless Georgia sun. Confederate guards sometimes shot Union prisoners without provocation, and in some cases, seemingly for sport.

By the war's end, nearly 13,000 Union soldiers had died within its palisades, making it the deadliest POW camp in American history.

At the center of this nightmare was Captain Henry Wirz, a Swiss-born Confederate officer whose leadership ranged from "grossly negligent" to "actively malevolent," depending on which survivor you asked. When the war ended, Wirz became one of only two men tried and executed for war crimes. His defense, essentially "I was just following orders" did not go over well with a nation still grieving its lost sons.

Yet, Andersonville's horrors might have been swallowed by history if not for men like Dorence Atwater, a Union POW ordered to record the names of the dead. Realizing his captors would likely destroy the official list, he made a secret copy: one of the boldest acts of bureaucratic rebellion ever undertaken with pen and ink. Thanks to him, thousands of families learned the fate of their missing loved ones. Another inmate, Newell Burch, kept a diary, chronicling the camp's grisly conditions in detail so raw you could almost smell the rot between the lines.

Even now, the moral calculus of Andersonville remains unsettling. Were the Confederate soldiers who stood guard merely following orders, or had they surrendered their humanity to war's numbing machinery? The question lingers like the ghosts of the men who perished there, a reminder that cruelty, when left unchecked, can transform ordinary places into something truly nightmarish.

— Further Reading —

Kantor, MacKinlay, *Andersonville*. Plume, 2016. [historical novel]

Chapter 91 Blue Hawaii

Let's get something clear right up front: Hawaii (it's now spelled *Hawai'i* but never mind that) didn't "join" the United States like a person volunteers for a potluck. No, Hawai'i was *annexed*—a five-dollar word that means "taken with a straight face and a crooked grin." And what the U.S. took wasn't just land and beaches, it was a full-blown, functioning kingdom. You know, the kind with a flag, a national anthem, and people who didn't ask to become extras in someone else's empire.

Back in the 19th century, Hawai'i had its own king: Kalākaua, a man so stylish he looked like he might've invented the sash. The place was sovereign, with elections and laws and all the stuff that makes a country a country, including the annoying parts like taxes. But that all got flushed down the historical toilet in 1887 when a bunch of white dudes with business cards and guns decided they were tired of being guests and would now be in charge of the house.

Enter the Bayonet Constitution, which sounds like a punk album but was actually a document drafted by sugar magnates who figured democracy worked best when only they got to vote. King Kalākaua was politely informed, at gunpoint, that he could either sign it or enjoy the hospitality of a nearby grave. He signed. Surprise! Suddenly, all the power shifted to a bunch of guys whose main qualifications were "owns a plantation" and "can spell 'republic.'"

Then, in 1893, the queen—Lili'uokalani, who played the long game and played it with grace—tried to fix it. She wanted to restore the constitution and give Hawaiians their government back. Aww. That's cute. Except she was immediately overthrown by the same local businessmen, now with U.S. Marines as backup dancers. The whole thing was so shady it needed sunscreen.

Five years later, in 1898, during the Spanish-American War (which started for reasons even historians describe as "murky at best"), Congress realized they could use Hawai'i as a convenient military outpost. So they just... took it. No treaty with the Hawaiian Kingdom, no vote by its people. It was like buying a house you don't own by declaring it "strategically valuable."

Fast forward to 1959, when Hawai'i became the 50th state. The ballot offered two options: "Would you like to be a state, or would you like to keep being a federally managed outpost with no representation?" Independence wasn't even on the menu. That's not democracy; that's a vending machine that only sells one flavor of chips.

And now? Now we get sanitized history tours, where the overthrow is a footnote and the monarchy is something that happened "a long time ago," right between the invention of hula and the arrival of the first ABC Store. The truth, as we have seen, is less charming: a kingdom was stolen in broad daylight by men in suits with rifles and agendas. What followed was decades of legislative gaslighting and tourist-friendly gloss.

But hey, at least you can get a piña colada while standing on the bones of a stolen kingdom.

— Further Reading —

Haley, James L., *Captive Paradise: A History of Hawaii*. St. Martin's Griffin, 2015.

Chapter 92 Play Football, Not War

The Christmas Truce of 1914 is one of the most remarkable and poignant moments in World War I history, showcasing a brief, unexpected pause in the violence that defined much of the war. It's a story of humanity shining through the horrors of conflict—of soldiers, who were enemies only days before, coming together in the spirit of the holiday, sharing stories, games, and even gifts.

Trench warfare had been established but was still in its early development. The static front had settled, but the trench systems were primitive compared to what would evolve later in the war. And on Christmas Eve, both sides—mainly British and German forces—began to halt their fighting spontaneously. It was small gestures at first such as soldiers putting up impromptu signs on either side of their trenches wishing one another "Merry Christmas" or singing carols to each other. The Germans apparently started with some Christmas carols, then the British joined in, furthermore contributing to the atmosphere for the truce by sharing this singing over the lines.

The military hierarchy did not plan the truce; instead, it was a soldier-initiated event. In many places along the front, soldiers emerged from their trenches into no-man's land; tentatively at first, but then more freely. They met halfway between the lines, shook hands, almost as if it were a family holiday. They showed pictures of their families to each other, emphasizing the human side of the opposing soldiers behind the guns. Some of the soldiers from both sides actually exchanged coats, little keepsakes, and talked about their home, hopes, and lives far away from the war.

And then? Well, in Whoville, they say that the Grinch's small heart grew three sizes that day.

Soldiers, in the more widely known areas of the front, organized spontaneous soccer games in the spirit of the Christmas truce. The games were generally informal with no organized field, goals, or rules, yet these games capture the spirit of the truce—human beings bonding together amid horrific violence, temporarily quelled. While the matches were friendly for the majority of the time, they also became an issue for tension because the officers in both armies were worried that their men were getting too cozy with the enemy.

Yet the truce was not everywhere nor for very long; military leaders became furious with this unexpected fraternization. They acted very quickly, sending some officers at the front to replace some soldiers with those who had taken part in the truce. In some cases, they even completely rotated out some battalions, fearing that the soldiers would find it hard to fight against each other since they had known one another during the short window of peace. Orders were also given to commence with fighting on December 26th, with usual hostilities back up in full swing in the following days. Even the higher-ups were so concerned about the unexpected incident on the field that they attempted to scale down or deny it, out of fear of giving the public an exaggerated idea of the war's reality.

This highly mercurial truce, however, became a symbol for the very possibility of peace even in very desperate circumstance. And it holds that these soldiers, when stripped of all titles of "enemy" or "combatant," could recognize their shared humanity and the senselessness of the war.

Through time, the truce was glamorized into a heart-rending scene of goodwill; nevertheless, it also rather pointed to psychological and moral stresses emanating from trench warfare. The reality is that the soldiers on both sides, most of whom were conscripted and had little or no personal animosity against one another, by a huge margin recognized that a temporary break from violence was needed.

Alas, it was a fleeting moment as the war would continue wreaking havoc for four more years. But the Christmas Truce remains probably one of the most touching stories of Great War; it teaches us that even in the darkest hour, mercy and companionship break through.

The French film *Joyeux Noël* (2005), Christian Carion's directorial work, dramatizes the events surrounding the 1914 Christmas Truce set against the backdrop of World War I. The story is related from several points of view: German, French, and Scottish soldiers, focusing on how they all came together in the spirit of Christmas to temporarily cease fighting and share the peaceful moment. The film shows how combatants of different backgrounds—and enemies until yesterday—bonded through carol singing, sharing of food, and even footballing together.

Joyeux Noël presents a heartbreaking portrayal of the truce filled with a moment of warmth with the brutal reality that followed, forcing the soldiers to engage in combat again, under pressure from their commanding officers. The film is an emotional yet powerful retelling of this wondrous event in history. It won several awards and was nominated for the Academy Award for Best Foreign Language Film.

— **Further Reading** —

Weintraub, Stanley, *Silent Night: The Story of the World War I Christmas Truce.* Plume, 2001.

(Artist's conception)

Chapter 93 Sniper vs. The Red Baron

Manfred von Richthofen, known to his friends and presumably his mom and dad as Manfred but to the rest of the world as The Red Baron, was not your run-of-the-mill World War I fighter pilot. He was a celestial executioner, a virtuoso of aerial combat, the grim reaper with a scarf and a bright red Fokker Dr.I triplane. By the time he was shot down in April 1918, he had accumulated 80 confirmed kills: a fact that, while deeply unsettling for his enemies, also forced them to tip their helmets (or, more likely, tin hats) in his direction.

When he finally met his end—possibly by an Australian machine gunner, possibly by friendly fire, or possibly just because physics and gravity are undefeated in the long run—his adversaries did something rather surprising: they buried him with full military honors. It was a stark reminder that, at the time, chivalry in warfare wasn't entirely dead, though it was gasping for breath somewhere in the trenches. While "The Great War" continued, French officers attended the ceremony and British and Australian pilots paid respects.

But history being history, there had to be controversy. The official explanation of who actually downed the Red Baron is a tangled mess of competing theories, national pride, and the fact that wartime eyewitness accounts are about as reliable as a drunk raccoon describing a UFO sighting. The Australians boasted that one of their soldiers got the shot (this is the accepted claim today), while the French, in an admirable display of national self-confidence, have put forth René Fonck, a man who was also an ace but had absolutely no direct connection to the event.[p] Then there's the argument that Canadian pilot Arthur Roy Brown played a role, possibly by forcing

---

[p] Fonck was the second most effective fighter pilot of WWI after von Richthofen.

von Richthofen into a position where ground fire got him. In short: the Baron went down, but the fight over *how* and by *whom* remains a bit airborne.

The Red Baron died not with fanfare, but with the inconvenient abruptness that often attends icons. Germany grieved, of course. That was expected. Less expected, perhaps, was how his enemies reacted: not with mockery, not even with war-hardened indifference, but with ceremonial decorum more suited to the death of a weary general than a 25-year-old ace brought down near the river Somme.

So on April 22, 1918, the Allies buried him as if he had been one of their own. The funeral, conducted near the village of Bertangles, was not some perfunctory gesture, but a full military affair, complete with officers standing in alignment, uniforms stiff with protocol, and a rifle salute delivered by the Australian Flying Corps. Wreaths arrived from nearby squadrons: floral arrangements that seemed almost embarrassed to speak of admiration in the language of petals.

It would not be his final grave.

Seven years later, in that uneasy period between wars (and before we learned we would need to start numbering them), as memory was already being reshaped for newer purposes, his youngest brother Bolko arrived to collect the body. One imagines the paperwork alone could have buried a less persistent man. The family, steeped in the tradition of tidy lineage and appropriate resting places, intended to have him laid beside their patriarch and Lothar, the other flying Richthofen, who had survived the war only to die in a plane crash during peacetime, as if the gods of aviation disliked being cheated.

But the German government, never one to miss an opportunity for pageantry, had other ideas. They lobbied for the Invalidenfriedhof in Berlin, a cemetery already overpopulated with uniforms, medals, and the sort of men who made history either by design or by accident. The family relented. And so Manfred von Richthofen, who had once turned the sky into a canvas of controlled aggression, was given a state funeral and buried among the architects and relics of German military ambition, still not his final resting place. Due to damage to his tombstone, there was one last move to the family grave location in Wiesbaden in 1975.

There he lies now, not merely as a fallen pilot, but as a cautionary figure of martial romance, embalmed in two layers of reverence: one private, one performed with solemn grandiosity.

And then there's "Snoopy vs. The Red Baron," the bizarre but delightful pop-cultural twist to this saga. Released in 1966 by The Royal Guardsmen, the song is a foot-stomping, entirely unserious retelling of a (very fictional) dogfight between Snoopy, Peanuts' aviation-obsessed beagle, and von Richthofen himself. In this alternate-history fever dream, the Red Baron, instead of facing the grim realities of war, squares off against a cartoon dog flying a weaponized doghouse. This, one assumes, is not how von Richthofen imagined his legacy.

The song was a monster hit, reaching #2 on the Billboard Hot 100, proving that Americans, despite being largely unfamiliar with World War I aviation history, could at least get behind a catchy tune about it. It was also the first in a series of Snoopy-themed war songs because apparently, once you've made a novelty hit about an Anthropomorphic beagle engaging in air-to-air combat while prone on his dog house, there's really nowhere to go but further into the absurd.

So, in sum: the Red Baron was a warrior-poet of the skies, his death remains a matter of debate, and he was later immortalized not through solemn war memorials but via a 1960s pop song about a beagle beating him in battle. History, as always, has a sense of humor.

— Further Reading —
Franks, Norman, and Bennett, Alan, *The Red Baron's Last Flight: A Mystery Investigated*. Grub Street Publishing, 2008.

— Easy Viewing —
"Blood Red: The Life and Death of Manfred von Richthofen."
www.youtube.com/watch?v=Q-prS5Izbic

Chapter 94 The Giant Panjandrum

The Out-of-Control Rocket Wheel

War produces many things: heroism, tragedy, and, every so often, an engineering catastrophe so staggeringly absurd that one must assume everyone involved was either deeply sleep-deprived or slightly insane. Enter the Giant Panjandrum, a British wartime invention that can best be described as what happens when someone tries to weaponize a rolling pin using pure madness and high explosives.

The idea, on paper, sounded almost reasonable, if you'd spent the last five years inhaling aircraft fuel. The Germans had fortified the French coastline with massive concrete defenses, and storming them head-on was a logistical nightmare. So, British engineers, presumably after several drinks, decided that the best solution was a giant, rocket-propelled wheel loaded with explosives, which would hurtle toward the enemy at breakneck speed and smash straight through their defenses.

Yes. A rocket-powered wheel of doom. Because when has strapping high-powered propulsion to an uncontrollable object ever gone wrong?

The First Test: A Case Study in Near-Homicide

The first real-world trial took place on a quiet English beach, where scientists, military officers, and at least one unfortunate dog gathered to witness history being made. And history was made; just not in the way anyone had hoped.

The moment the 36 solid-fuel rockets ignited, the Panjandrum lurched forward, hesitated, then began a terrifying, chaotic rampage across the sand. It did not go straight. It did not go left. It did not go right. It simply went berserk, careening unpredictably like a drunken carnival ride gone rogue.

Observers, many of whom were high-ranking British officers, ran for their lives. A senior naval official was nearly flattened. The dog, smarter than any of the humans present, fled immediately. Meanwhile, the Panjandrum, utterly indifferent to its own mission, veered off course, shed several of its rockets mid-roll, and eventually collapsed in a heap of failure, its remaining rockets still hissing in what one can only assume was deep mechanical humiliation.

Subsequent Tests: More Rockets, More Chaos, Same Result

Undeterred by this magnificent disaster, the engineers tried again. And again. And again. Each time, the Panjandrum's performance ranged from "mildly catastrophic" to "good God, who let this thing out of the lab?" Rockets detached mid-spin, sending fiery projectiles in random directions. The wheel flipped, tumbled, and on one occasion, attacked the film crew recording the test.

At no point did it ever travel in a straight line toward a target.

Eventually, someone in the British military—probably after nearly being run down by their own weapon—had the good sense to call the whole thing off. The Giant Panjandrum was quietly abandoned, presumably with an agreement never to speak of it again.

A Legacy of Lunacy

The name "Panjandrum," a nonsense word invented by 18th-century actor and writer Samuel Foote, was, in hindsight, astonishingly accurate, as the original word referred to something bombastic or overbearing. This was a machine that defied logic, ignored physics, and did its absolute best to assassinate anyone foolish enough to be near it. It was an engineering marvel in the sense that it's marvelous it didn't kill half the British high command.

Today, the Giant Panjandrum stands as one of the greatest (and funniest) cautionary tales of military invention. It remains a shining, rocket-propelled monument to desperation, bad ideas, and the eternal truth that just because something can be built doesn't mean it should be.[40][41]

Chapter 95 Bat Bombs

There are bad ideas, and then there are *Bat Bombs*. Yes, you read that right. The United States military—those stalwart defenders of liberty, freedom, and the occasional inexplicable technical misstep—seriously entertained the idea of using bats to deliver bombs during World War II. The concept came courtesy of Lytle S. Adams, a dentist who, it seems, was quite literally trying to sink his teeth into military strategy. Adams—who clearly had more ideas than sense—proposed a plan so absurd that even the most seasoned war planners must have briefly wondered if they were being pranked.

The plan was simple: take a bunch of bats, attach incendiary bombs to them, and then release them over Japan. The idea, called "Project X-Ray," was that these creepy little agents of destruction would roost in the attics of houses and set them on fire, creating mass chaos. It sounds like something out of an old Batman episode, with Adam West donning a cape made entirely of shredded bat wings and attempting to stop a crime wave with his "Bat-bomb-astically" misguided sense of justice.

And yet, against all odds, the U.S. military went ahead with testing, because, well, sometimes it's hard to resist the allure of a truly insane idea, especially when the alternative is something boring, like regular bombs. But bats do not make great bombers. They have a tendency to fly off in any direction but the one you intend. The result? A lot of bats set free, some misguided military officers chasing them down, and no fiery destruction of enemy targets.

In the end, Project X-Ray was shut down after numerous failed—and even disastrous—tests. But for a brief moment in history, it looked as though we might owe the end of WWII to the world's most unlikely delivery system: bats with bombs attached. Had it worked, we might all be reading about how Bat Bombs ended the war in *literally* the most unexpected way possible. Instead, the whole thing was filed under "Things That Should Have Stayed In A Batcave"—a strange experiment that's mostly forgotten, but in its own way, a triumph of imagination over practicality.[42]

But I know what you're thinking: "Bats? That's crazy. *Pigeons* are the way to go"...

— Further Reading —

Glines, Carroll V., *Air and Space Forces*. "The Bat Bombers." Oct 1990. www.airandspaceforces.com/article/1090bats/

Chapter 96 Pigeon-Guided Missiles

That's right, forget the "bats" idea. It is difficult to overstate just how bonkers this next idea was. They chose the top secret code name "Project Pigeon," perhaps because "Project X-Ray" was already taken.

So at some point during World War II, a room full of allegedly serious military professionals looked at each other and said, "You know what would really improve our missile guidance systems? Birds." And not just any birds: pigeons, a species known primarily for its ability to deface public monuments and fly directly into glass windows.

This marvel of military ingenuity was dreamed up by B.F. Skinner, a man who made his career studying behavior modification and presumably thought, "If I can get rats to press a lever, I can certainly train pigeons to operate a missile." The theory was straightforward: stuff a pigeon inside the missile's guidance system, have it peck at an image of a target, and let the resulting pecks guide the weapon of destruction. If this sounds like something out of a rejected Looney Tunes script, congratulations—you have not been permanently desensitized to government spending. "Powerhouse" by Raymond Scott should now be playing in your head. It is in mine.

And yet, it worked. The pigeons, being pigeons, were utterly unbothered by their role in this death-delivery system. As long as they got their food pellets, they would enthusiastically peck away at enemy battleships or unsuspecting supply depots. If there had been a Nobel Prize for 'Most Deranged Yet Functionally Sound Wartime Scheme,' Skinner would have been a shoo-in.

Alas, the project was eventually scrapped, not because it didn't work, but because some bureaucrat, in a rare moment of clarity, realized that basing national defense on animals with a brain the size of a peanut might not inspire public confidence. And so, Skinner's pigeons were honorably discharged, free to return to a life of dive-bombing park benches and performing whatever sinister tasks they actually spend their time on when we're not looking.

— Further Reading —

Stromberg, Joseph, *Smithsonian Magazine*, "B.F. Skinner's Pigeon-Guided Rocket." August 18, 2011.
  www.smithsonianmag.com/smithsonian-institution/bf-skinners-pigeon-guided-rocket-53443995/

Chapter 97 Surviving Atomic Explosions

Oh, What a Lucky, Unlucky Man He Was

There is bad luck, and then there is Tsutomu Yamaguchi-level bad luck—a kind of statistical aberration so perverse it makes you question whether the universe is simply incompetent or actively malevolent. The man survived not one, but two nuclear bombings—which sounds less like a biography and more like a Kafkaesque fever dream written by someone who had spent too much time licking uranium.

It began, as these things often do, with a business trip. Yamaguchi, a Mitsubishi engineer, was in Hiroshima when the first bomb fell. The plane appears, the bomb drops, and suddenly he's partially deaf, half-burned, and standing in the wreckage of what had previously been a functioning city. He staggers through the apocalyptic landscape, past firestorms, melting infrastructure, and people who have just discovered what it feels like to be both alive and dead at the same time. Most rational individuals would consider this a fairly conclusive reason to take a sick day. Yamaguchi, however, gets on a train.

Yes. A train. Running through the ruins of Hiroshima. On schedule. One can only assume that Japanese rail punctuality is some kind of immutable law of physics, immune even to nuclear warfare. Destination? Nagasaki, of course, because there is no conceivable way this story is allowed to end here.

And sure enough, two days later, while he's in his boss's office, explaining why he might be running a little behind schedule, Nagasaki explodes. Again. At this point, one must assume that somewhere, a celestial bureaucrat is furiously flipping through paperwork, realizing some kind of clerical error has occurred. But Yamaguchi, like some kind of war-torn Wile E. Coyote, survives this one too.

This man lived to 93 years old. He had children. He outlived the century that tried, repeatedly, to kill him. And in his later years, he spent time campaigning against nuclear weapons, presumably because after personally experiencing 100% of their battlefield usage, he had formed a fairly solid opinion on the subject.

Was Yamaguchi the luckiest man alive, or had he simply reached a point where luck, whether good or bad, had nothing to do with it? That's the trouble with history: it refuses to be clean, or simple, or reasonable. But at least we know one thing: if the apocalypse ever does come, somewhere out there, a train will still be running on time.[43]

Chapter 98 A Monopoly Game Of Mass Escape

When Passing GO Meant Getting The Hell Out.

Listen up, people! While you were using Monopoly to destroy family relationships at Christmas, British intelligence—specifically the ultra-clandestine MI9 division—was turning it into James Bond's emergency escape kit in a box.

During World War II, British intelligence operatives—apparently having watched too many spy movies but *actually making it work*—partnered with Waddington's, the UK Monopoly manufacturer, to create the world's most consequential "special edition" board game since forever. These weren't your standard "Star Wars Edition" or "City of Cleveland " or "Spanish Inquisition" variants. These were the "escape from Nazi Germany before they shoot you" edition.

Here's how this absolutely insane scheme worked: Special Monopoly sets reportedly included a subtle marker, like a dot or mark on the Free Parking space, which, let's face it, is normally the most useless space in the game unless your family plays with those made-up rules where you get all the tax money. The Red Cross delivered these games to POW camps where captured Allied airmen immediately recognized the signal (assuming they'd been briefed before getting shot down, which wasn't always a guarantee—"military intelligence" being occasionally just *military*).

Inside these miracle boxes? The cardboard game boards concealed actual escape maps printed on silk—because paper maps make noise and fall apart when wet, problems that anyone who's tried to refold a gas station map while driving certainly appreciates. The metal game tokens hid tiny working compasses. And the kicker? Real French, German, and Italian currency hidden among the pink, blue, and yellow Monopoly money!

The Germans never caught on. While they were checking food packages for hidden rasp files, they completely ignored the games that *were literally designed to help people get out of jail.*

This classified operation remained secret until half a century later, when the British government finally admitted that while most of us were just trying to build hotels on Boardwalk, they were using Parker Brothers' capitalist fantasy to conduct the greatest prison break program in military history. And you thought landing on Park Place with a hotel was stressful!⁴⁴

(Artist's conception)

Chapter 99 Maginot Line

The *Maginot Line* is what happens when you give military planners too much money and not enough imagination. It was, in essence, France's very expensive way of saying, "Well, that should do it."

Between 1929 and 1938, the French built a 3-billion-franc super fortress along their border with Germany, presumably under the assumption that the Germans, out of some sense of sportsmanship, would only attack from the direction they were expected to. The Maginot Line had everything: massive underground bunkers, air-conditioned barracks, turrets that could rise out of the ground like some kind of medieval fever dream, and enough concrete to make a modern city planner weep with envy. What it did not have, unfortunately, was a plan for what to do if the Germans just ignored it.

Which, of course, they did. Because why wouldn't they? The Maginot Line was the military equivalent of building a 20-foot-high fence around your front yard while leaving the back door wide open. In May 1940, when the Germans decided to invade France, they didn't even bother trying to punch through the Maginot Line. Instead, the Germans executed a brilliant feint through Belgium, while their main forces surged through the Ardennes, an area the French had considered impassable to tanks, and proceeded to take France apart like a poorly assembled IKEA shelf.

By June, the French army was in full panic mode, and the Maginot Line stood there almost completely untouched, like an extremely well-fortified relic of a war that never happened. Some French soldiers were actually forced to retreat into the very fortifications that were supposed to keep the enemy out, which is like buying a state-of-the-art security system and then moving into the panic room permanently. Yet the Line itself did accomplish its job. It was France's assumptions about where the job would be that fell apart.

In the grand history of deeply regrettable military investments, the Maginot Line sits somewhere between the Trojan Horse incident and any country's attempt to invade Russia in winter. It was an engineering marvel, a logistical masterpiece, and a stunningly misguided monument to human optimism. And today, it serves as an enduring reminder that when preparing for the next big threat, it's best to make sure it's not the one you already survived.

A wooden fence and a "Keep Out" sign would have worked almost as well. But should the sign be in French, or in German?

Bibliography

Baker, William Avery, *The Pilgrim Colony: A History of New Plymouth, 1620–1691*. Yale University Press, 1961.

Ballard, J. G., *The Wind as a Tool: Theo Jansen's Strandbeest Project*. MIT Press, 2017.

Bartholomew, Robert E., *Little Green Men, Meowing Nuns and Head-Hunting Panics: A Study of Mass Psychogenic Illness and Social Delusion*. McFarland, 2001.

Baxter, Stephen, and David Atkinson, *Tunguska: The Final Answer*. Faber & Faber, 2013.

Bell, Michelle L., et al., "A Retrospective Assessment of Mortality from the London Smog Episode of 1952: The Role of Influenza and Pollution." *Environmental Health Perspectives* 112, no. 1 (2004): 6–8.

Behringer, Wolfgang, *Witchcraft Persecutions in Bavaria: Popular Magic, Religious Zealotry, and Reason of State in Early Modern Europe*. Cambridge University Press, 1997.

Bradbrook, Bohuslav, *Karel Čapek: In Pursuit of Truth, Tolerance, and Trust*. Sussex Academic Press, 1998.

Brimblecombe, Peter, *The Big Smoke: A History of Air Pollution in London since Medieval Times*. Routledge, 1987.

Browning, Robert, *The Pied Piper of Hamelin*. London, 1842.

Brumbaugh, Robert S., *The Most Mysterious Manuscript: The Voynich "Roger Bacon" Cipher Manuscript*. Southern Illinois University Press, 1978.

Capelotti, P. J., *By Airship to the North Pole: An Archaeology of Human Exploration*. Rutgers University Press, 1999.

Capron, Michel, *L'Affaire de Pont-Saint-Esprit: Une Enquête Inédite*. L'Harmattan, 2008.

Carlson, W. Bernard, *Tesla: Inventor of the Electrical Age*. Princeton University Press, 2013.

Catholic Encyclopedia, first edition. The Encyclopedia Press, 1907-1913.

Cepl, Petr, *Karel Čapek: Life and Work*. Artia, 1965.

Cooke, William, *Justice at Salem*. Undertaker Press, 2014.

Darnton, Robert, *The Great Cat Massacre: and Other Episodes in French Cultural History*. Basic Books, 2009.

De Camp, L. Sprague, *The Ancient Engineers*. New York: Ballentine Books, 1960.

Dikötter, Frank, *Mao's Great Famine: The History of China's Most Devastating Catastrophe, 1958–1962*. Walker & Company, 2010.

DiSimone, Anthony, *The Devil's Bread: Ergotism and the Mass Poisoning at Pont-Saint-Esprit*. Palgrave Macmillan, 2016.

Evans, C.J., *The Great Emu War: Or How Australia Lost A War Against Birds*. (Independently published) 2018.

Eyman, Scott, *Lion of Hollywood: The Life and Legend of Louis B. Mayer*. Simon & Schuster, 2005.

Farazmand, Ali (ed.), *Handbook of Crisis and Emergency Management*. New York: Marcel Decker, 2001.

Farman, Irvin, *Tandy's Money Machine: How Charles Tandy Built Radio Shack into the World's Largest Electronics Chain*. Mobium Pr, 1993.

Feynman, Richard P., *"What Do You Care What Other People Think?": Further Adventures of a Curious Character*. W.W. Norton & Company, 1988.

Fiore, Tony, *The Corvair Decade: An Illustrated History of the Rear Engined Automobile*. Corvair Society of America, 1980.

Fowler, George, et. al., *Car-tastrophes: 80 Automotive Atrocities from the past 20 years*. Veloce, 2020.

Fullagar, Kate, *The Mass Poisoning at Pont-Saint-Esprit: Madness in a French Town*. Bloomsbury, 2022.

Gendron, Josée, *La grande escroquerie du sirop d'érable*. Les Éditions La Presse, 2013.

Goldstone, Lawrence, *Birdmen: The Wright Brothers, Glenn Curtiss, and the Battle to Control the Skies*. Ballantine Books, 2014.

Green, Bobby, *Gone at 3:17: The Untold Story of the Worst School Disaster in American History*. University of Texas Press, 2012.

Greenberg, Joel, *A Feathered River Across the Sky: The Passenger Pigeon's Flight to Extinction*. Bloomsbury, 2014.

Hagerty, Jack, and Rogers, Jon C., *Spaceship Handbook*. ARA Press, 2001.

Haley, James L., *Captive Paradise: A History of Hawaii*. St. Martin's Griffin, 2015.

Harmetz, Aljean, *The Making of The Wizard of Oz: Movie Magic and Studio Power in the Prime of MGM—and the Miracle of Production #1060*. Delta, 1984.

Haught, James A., *Holy Horrors*. Amherst: Prometheus, 2002.

Hempelmann, Christian F., "The laughter of the 1962 Tanganyika 'laughter epidemic'." *HUMOR: International Journal of Humor Research*. Walter de Gruyter, 2007.

Hermelin, Beate, *Bright Splinters of the Mind: A Personal Story of Research with Autistic Savants*. Jessica Kingsley Publishers, 2001.

Horner, Lana, *Banqiao Dam Failure: The Collapse That Cost Thousands of Lives.* (Independently published) 2024.

Jackson, Lee, *Dirty Old London: The Victorian Fight Against Filth*. Yale University Press, 2014.

Jansen, Theo, *Strandbeest: The Dream Machines of Theo Jansen*. Taschen, 2016.

Jones, Christopher, *Great Palace: Story of Parliament*. BBC Books, 1983.

Kantor, MacKinlay, *Andersonville*. Plume, 2016.

Kitz, Janet F., *Shattered City: The Halifax Explosion and the Road to Recovery*. Nimbus Publishing, 1989.

Kride, E. L., *The Tunguska Meteorite*: An Eye-Witness Account. Progress Publishers, 1967.

Lee, Seungho, *China's Water Resources Management: A Long March to Sustainability*. Palgrave Macmillan, 2014.

Lees-Milne, James, *Building St. Peter's: The Construction of the New Basilica of St. Peter's in Rome, 1506–1626*. Faber and Faber, 1974.

Lehto, Steve, *Preston Tucker and His Battle to Build the Car of Tomorrow*. Chicago Review Press, 2018.

Levack, Brian, *The Witch-Hunt in Early Modern Europe*. New York: Longman, 1995.

Leveson, Nancy G. *Safeware: System Safety and Computers*. Addison-Wesley, 1995.

Lewis, Brenda, *A Dark History: The Popes*. New York: Metro Books, 2009.

Lietzmann, Hans, *A History of the Early Church*. Cleveland and New York: Meridian Books, 1961.

Mackay, Charles, *Extraordinary Popular Delusions and the Madness of Crowds*. New York: Harmony, 1980.

Macmillan, Malcolm. *An Odd Kind of Fame: Stories of Phineas Gage*. MIT Press, 2000.

Marchant, Jo, *Decoding the Heavens: A 2000-Year-Old Computer—and the Century-Long Search to Discover Its Secrets*. Da Capo Press, 2009.

Martin, Thomas R., Rosenwein, Barbara H., Smith, Bonnie G., *The Making of the West, Combined Volume: Peoples and Cultures*. Boston: Bedford/St. Martin's, 2012.

McCarthy, Michael, *The Hidden Hindenburg: The Untold Story of the Tragedy, the Nazi Secrets, and the Quest to Rule the Skies.* Lyons Press, 2020.

McCullough, David, *The Johnstown Flood*. Simon & Schuster, 1987.

McCullough, David, *The Wright Brothers*. Simon & Schuster, 2016.

Medvedev, Zhores. *Nuclear Disaster in the Urals.* W. W. Norton & Company, 1980.

Markel, Howard, *The Kelloggs: The Battling Brothers of Battle Creek*. Vintage, 2018.

Mieder, Wolfgang, *The Pied Piper: A Handbook*. Westport, Connecticut, 2007.

Mikaberidze, Alexander, *Atrocities, Massacres, and War Crimes: An Encyclopedia*. Santa Barbara: ABC-CLIO, 2013.

Morris, Charles R. *The Tycoons: How Andrew Carnegie, John D. Rockefeller, Jay Gould, and J.P. Morgan Invented the American Supereconomy*. New York: Times Books, 2010.

Myers, Philip Van Ness, *Mediaeval and Modern History*. Cambridge: Athenium Press, 1905.

NASA, "Columbia Crew Survival Investigation Report." NASA/SP-2008-565, December 30, 2008.

Neufeld, Michael J., *The Rocket and the Reich*. Smithsonian Books, 2013.

O'Callaghan, Timothy J., *The Aviation Legacy of Henry & Edsel Ford*. First Page Publications, 2001.

O'Loughlin, Thomas, *Saint Patrick: The Man and his Works*. London: S.P.C.K., 1999.

Oxford Encyclopedia of Women in World History. Bonnie G. Smith, ed. New York: Oxford University Press, 2008.

Paulkovich, Michael, *Beyond the Crusades : Christianity's lies, laws, and legacy*, 2023.

Paulkovich, Michael, *Mostly Harmful: 1001 Things Everyone Should Know About Religion*, 2025.

Pawle, Gerald, *The Wheezers and Dodgers: The Inside Story of Clandestine Weapon Development in World War II*. Seaforth Publishing, 2009.

Pearson, Charles T., *Indomitable Tin Goose: A Biography of Preston Tucker*. Pocket, 1988.

Pendergrast, Mark, *For God, Country, and Coca-Cola*. Basic Books, 2013.

Perrow, Charles. *Normal Accidents: Living with High-Risk Technologies*. Princeton University Press, 1984.

Philbrick, Nathaniel. *Mayflower: A Story of Courage, Community, and War*. Viking, 2006.

Postma, Johannes, *The Atlantic Slave Trade*. London: Greenwood Press, 2003.

Pyke, Josh. *Explosion in Halifax Harbour: The Illustrated History of a Disaster That Shook the World*. Formac Publishing, 1994.

Randolph, Marc, *That Will Never Work: The Birth of Netflix and the Amazing Life of an Idea*. Back Bay Books, 2019.

Richler, Mordecai. *The Great Canadian Maple Syrup Heist: How a Sticky Caper Changed Quebec's Sweetest Industry*. Random House Canada, 2015.

Robbins, Rossell Hope, *The Encyclopedia of Witchcraft and Demonology*. New York: Crown, 1959.

Robinson, Douglas H, and Charles L. Keller. *"Up Ship!": U.S. Navy Rigid Airships 1919–1935*. Annapolis, Maryland: United States Naval Institute, 1982,

Russell, Jeffrey Burton, *Witchcraft in the Middle Ages*. Ithaca: Cornell University Press, 1984.

Sandström, Birgitta. *Vasa: The Story of a Swedish Warship*. Collins, 1988.

Schechter, Harold. *The Serial Killer Files: The Who, What, Where, How, and Why of the World's Most Terrifying Murderers*. Ballantine Books, 2003.

Schorger, A. W. *The Passenger Pigeon: Its Natural History and Extinction*. University of Wisconsin Press, 1955.

Seifer, Marc J. Wizard: *The Life and Times of Nikola Tesla*. Citadel Press, 1996.

Shales, Tom, and Miller, James Andrew, *Live From New York: The Complete, Uncensored History of Saturday Night Live as Told by Its Stars, Writers, and Guests*. Back Bay Books, 2015.

Shapiro, Judith. *Mao's War Against Nature: Politics and the Environment in Revolutionary China*. Cambridge University Press, 2001.

Simon, Robert I., *Bad Men Do What Good Men Dream*. Arlington: American Psychiatric Publishing, 2008.

Skinner, Stephen, *The Voynich Manuscript: The Complete Edition of the World' Most Mysterious and Esoteric Codex*. Watkins Publishing, 2017.

Stephanson, Anders, *Manifest Destiny: American Expansion and the Empire of Right*. New York: Hill and Wang, 1995.

Tammet, Daniel. *Born on a Blue Day: Inside the Extraordinary Mind of an Autistic Savant*. Free Press, 2007.

Tarshis, Lauren, *I Survived the Hindenburg Disaster, 1937*. Scholastic, 2016.

Treffert, Darold A. *Islands of Genius: The Bountiful Mind of the Autistic, Acquired, and Sudden Savant*. Jessica Kingsley Publishers, 2010.

Temporini, Hildegard, *Aufstieg und Niedergang der Römischen Welt*. Berlin: Walter de Gruyter, 1986.

Tronzo, William, ed. *St. Peter's in the Vatican*. Cambridge University Press, 2005.

Van Booy, Simon. *Rolls-Royce Motor Cars: Making a Legend*. ACC Art Books, 2020.

Walker, Barbara, *The Women's Encyclopedia of Myths and Secrets*. New York: HarperOne, 1983.

Waller, John, *A Time to Dance, a Time to Die: The Extraordinary Story of the Dancing Plague of 1518*. London: Icon Books, 2008.

Warnock, C. Gayle, *The Edsel affair: .... what went wrong? : A narrative.* Pro West, 1980.

Wegener, Herr Danny, *Rolls-Royce: The Pinnacle of Automotive Luxury.* (Independently published) 2025.

Weintraub, Stanley, *Silent Night: The Story of the World War I Christmas Truce.* Plume, 2001.

West, Gladys B., *It Began With A Dream.* Igwest Publishing, 2020.

Wilkman, Jon. *Floodpath: The Deadliest Man-Made Disaster of 20th-Century America and the Making of Modern Los Angeles.* Bloomsbury Press, 2016.

Wohl, Anthony S., *Endangered Lives: Public Health in Victorian Britain.* Harvard University Press, 1983.

END NOTES

1 For details, see Waller, and Bartholomew in the bibliography.

2 Postma, loc. cit.

3 *Nouvel Obs*, "En 1951, un village français a-t-il été arrosé de LSD par la CIA?" 2010.

4 Cooke.

5 *CNN*, Seth MacFarlane interview with Piers Morgan, September 11, 2011.

6 Rottman, Gordon L. *Military History*, "Operation Paul Bunyan." October 2001.

7 Levack, 41-42.

8 *Catholic Encyclopedia,* vol. 1, 268.

9 Mackay, 474.

10 Paulkovich, *Beyond the Crusades,* 113-114.

11 *Catholic Encyclopedia,* vol. 14, 283-284.

12 *Radair*, "Automotive Fun Fact: World's Highest Speeding Fines." August 28, 2013.

13 *iltalehti* newspaper.

14 Lee, Alexander, *History Today*, "Pigs Might Try." Vol. 70 Issue 11, Nov 2020.

15 Kieckhefer, Richard. *Medieval Magic: A Book of Essays*. Garland, 2000.

16 Althoff, Gerd. *Family, Friends and Followers: Political and Social Bonds in Early Medieval Europe*. Cambridge University Press, 2004.

17 *UK Parliament*, "The Great Fire of 1834."

18 Robinson, Douglas H.

19 Patowary, Kushik, *Amusing Planet*. "The Lake Peigneur Drilling Disaster." April 4, 2022.

20 Leveson, Nancy, 530-532.

21 Sardesai, Vinod, *Encyclopedia of Cleveland History*, "Balloonfest." 2023.

22 *Department of Transport, London, HMSO*, "Report on the accident to Boeing 737-400 G-OBME near Kegworth, Leicestershire on 8 January 1989, Aircraft Accident Report 4/90, Air Accidents Investigation Branch." 25 August 1990.

23 Edelman, Alan, *SIAM Review*. "The Mathematics of the Pentium Division Bug," Vol. 39, No. 1, March 1997.

²⁴ Farazmand, 507-511.

²⁵ MacFarlane said that while writing the pilot episode for the show, he was reading *The Wright Brothers* by David McCullough and the name "Orville" seemed "like a good fit for our midlevel craft."

²⁶ Bendici, Ray, *Connecticut Today*. "Gustave Whitehead First to Fly? Maybe. Will His Fairfield House Crash?" April 15, 2024.

²⁷ *Catholic Encyclopedia*, vol. 11, 559.

²⁸ See also O'Loughlin.

²⁹ See also: Mieder; and Browning.

³⁰ *Star Talk*, "What's Up With That Square Structure on Mars", Feb 13, 2025

³¹ See Warnock.

³² "Tesla's Cybertruck Is The Auto Industry's Biggest Flop In Decades," retrieved April 8, 2025. www.youtube.com/watch?v=46bOzXx2iZI

³³ National Highway Traffic Safety Administration (NHTSA) Report, 1972—after a multi-year investigation, NHTSA concluded that the first-generation Corvair (1960–1963) was no more dangerous than its peers.

³⁴ "Sony Corp. of America v. Universal City Studios, Inc.," 464 U.S. 417 (1984).

³⁵ *CDO Times*, "Case Study: Kodak's Downfall—A Lesson in Failed Digital Transformation and Missed Opportunities."

³⁶ ycharts.com/companies/GOOG/market_cap (retrieved June 21, 2025).

³⁷ Doyle, Eóin, *Driven to Write*. "Sliding Doors – 2004 Peugeot 1007." 3 July 2017.

³⁸ *CBS News*, "Toyota 'Unintended Acceleration' Has Killed 89." May 25, 2010.

³⁹ *CBS Mornings*, "Youngest self-made female billionaire takes high-tech approach to blood testing." www.youtube.com/watch?v=UiNFXcI9Rb8 retrieved June 26, 2025.

⁴⁰ *IWM*, "Second World War Weapons That Failed."

⁴¹ See Pawle.

⁴² Christen, Arden G., and Christen, Joan A., *Pubmed*. "Dr. Lytle Adams' incendiary "bat bomb" of World War II." Nov 2004.

⁴³ McEvoy, Colin, *Biography*, "Tsutomu Yamaguchi: The Man Who Miraculously Survived Both Atomic Bombings." July 18, 2023.

⁴⁴ McMahon, Brian, *CNN*. "How board game helped free POWs." Dec 7, 2007.

www.ingramcontent.com/pod-product-compliance
Lightning Source LLC
Chambersburg PA
CBHW060455030426
42337CB00015B/1597